Your ADAM
IS ASLEEP UNTIL GOD
Opens His Eyes

Your ADAM IS ASLEEP UNTIL GOD *Opens His Eyes*

CONVERSATIONS BETWEEN A *Mother* AND *her daughters* ABOUT MEN.

BY DR. VELMA BAGBY

XULON PRESS

Xulon Press
2301 Lucien Way #415
Maitland, FL 32751
407.339.4217
www.xulonpress.com

Printed in the United States of America.

ISBN-13: 978-1-54563-792-0

Dedication

I gratefully acknowledge:

God for giving, leading and trusting me
with this inspired assignment.

My Daughters Elvie Tampol and Taylor Bagby. The words
"thank you" seems too insignificant to express the magnitude
of my appreciation for you two. You are every chapter, page
and word in this book. This book exists because of you and
your encouragement. Thank you for our conversations and
for your permission to share it with others.

My Husband and Pastor, Bruce Bagby, True Foundation
Ministries, San Pablo, CA
Thank you, Husband! I appreciate your encouragement and
support. Your words of encouragement were the motivation I
needed during the final push toward the finish line.

My Son-in-law Kris Tampol, Nindja Gear Company.
Son, thank you for your multimedia prowess;
your knowledge and expertise in this arena is second
to none. Your help was and is invaluable to me.

Dr. Yvonne Farr, Chancellor/Founder, Farr West Theological Seminary/Sacramento Theological Seminary Bible College. Thank you, Dr. Farr. You are part of this journey and the reason I considered writing. You are a true friend and teacher.

Elder Michele Brown, Wordplay Consulting. Thank you, Sis. Your expertise is priceless. The help you provided me is now permanent ornaments of beauty in this book. I appreciate your support.

I appreciate and acknowledge my other friends & supporters: Minister Marjorie Dansby, True Foundation Ministries, San Pablo, CA. Pastor Boaston Woodson and the Resurrection AME family of Richmond, CA. Lady Demetria Foster, now with the Lord.

Acknowledgements

Divine revelation and inspiration for anything concerning the thoughts and heart of God can only come from Him. God alone, gets all the glory and praise for this kingdom assignment. I am grateful for His leading at every step.

Dr. Velma Bagby

Forward

I n this day and time when women are no longer groomed for marriage, this book is the perfect guideline. Your Adam Is Asleep Until God Opens His Eyes book is for women at all stages of singleness; i.e., single never married, single divorcee, single parent. This book will truly open your eyes to new principles which teach you how to wait on God to bring your mate. You will find yourselves asking the question, Am I really ready? So, I ask you, what are you doing to prepare? My answer, read this book.

Mrs. Elvene' "Elvie" Tampol, Registered Nurse
Velma's elder daughter

I hope this book blesses others as much as experiencing the conversations and lessons blessed me. Reading this book brought me back to each and every moment and reminded me how impactful the conversations have been in my life. On this journey I learned it is not always about the other person, but it is about what God wants to change in you; and this is exactly what the lessons and experiences in the book provided me.

I complained about men being slow, but I was nowhere near ready and completely immature. But, with the direction and teachings mentioned in this book, I feel ready, more than ever before. I have watched myself change, grow and let go. It took a lot of tears, and a ton of pride I had to throw out the window. I had to fully give God all of me so He could lead me, not only to my Adam, but to my purpose in His kingdom.

As you read this book, it will take you on a journey which will not be easy but is very rewarding. I pray as you read this book, God will lead you just as He did me.

I honestly do not know who I would have become without what is imprinted in this book; and I really do not care to know. What I do know? Because of this book, I am blessed and truly grateful to be the woman I am today. A woman who now walks by faith, trusts God more than ever, and whose life was enriched through a process which started with honest, straightforward conversations with my Mother.

Taylor Bagby, Registered Nurse
Velma's younger daughter

Endorsements

I cannot thoroughly express how blessed and proud I am of Dr. Velma Bagby. I watched Dr. Bagby labor to bring this book, an important tool for the kingdom, into fruition. Your Adam Is Asleep Until God Opens His Eyes was destined to make its arrival in 2018; and in this season, is a much-needed resource for believers today. This book will benefit singles, married couples and I recommend this tool for single and married ministries.

Dr. Yvonne Farr, Chancellor/Founder of
Farr West Theological Seminary/Sacramento Theological
Seminary Bible College

If you truly want to know the difference between a contractual marriage versus a covenantal one, Your Adam Is Asleep Until God Opens His Eyes will educate you on the difference. As a single woman, I was extremely interested in reading this book to find out why men could not see a good thing standing in front of them. It wasn't until I read this book I understood men first must have a relationship with God, and then he'll be able to see and recognize the good in you. As a single woman, I also came to understand I was married to God until he arrives. Based on what I learned from this book, it is my duty to allow God to prepare the Eve "in me". What I love about this book is the variety of tools and guidelines to aid you in preparing and understanding the importance of waiting on your God sent mate. If you are a woman who is single or married and you are seeking to understand the Eve "in you" while waiting for your Adam to wake-up for the first, second or even the third time, I recommend you read Your Adam Is Asleep Until God Opens His Eyes.

Shonta Archie,
Founder Vanity Saks
Co-Founder B.E.A.U.T.Y. Scholars

Table of Contents

Introduction xvii

Chapter 1   Marriage Is Not Man Made, But
             God Made. 1
             Back to the Beginning
             The First of the Two Gardens
             God Owns the Patent for Marriage
             Marriage in the Bible, A Book 5 Billion Strong

Chapter 2   The First Man Adam Was Asleep 5
             Asleep or Slow
             Adam Was Alone, But Was Not Lonely
             Adam, the First Real Alpha Male
             A Man Who Prays and Listens

Chapter 3   The First Woman Was Called Good 13
             The Woman Made What Was Not Good, Good!
             She Was Not a Temporary Title
             The Helper Who Helps Lead

Chapter 4   Eve Was Adam's Missing Rib. 19
             The Man's Lost Rib
             Adam Gave His Rib So Eve Could Exist
             The Rib Must Return and You Are His
             Missing Rib
             Let Him Find His Good Thing

Chapter 5   **Intimacy in the Garden**............... **29**
The Second Garden
The Exciting Beauty of Discovery
A Couple with Purpose
The Two Were One Before They Were Two
The Two Became One Physically
Going Deeper, The Blood Covenant
"C" is for Celibacy
Adam Replacements, Batteries Not Included

Chapter 6   **More About Man, Warnings
and Dangers**....................... **45**
Like Adam, A Man Is on the Job
A Man Who Loves God, Knows How to Love
A Man at Dust Level is Not Ready
Warning! Spouse Fixer Upper or Animal
Rescue is Not a Wife's Job
Another Warning! Temps, Boys, and Boos
Watch Out for Counterfeits
Men Do Not Marry Their Toys
Men Can See Where You Are

Chapter 7   **Before I Do, Focus on You** **59**
Focus on You
Time for Preparation
Dating in Secret Ignores Wise Counsel
Poor Choices Result in a Mate from the Trash
or Falling in Love with a Dog
Do Not Be the Woman from the Poop Pile
Do Not Be the Woman A Man Cannot Lift
the Covers On
Do Not Be A Man's Toy

Chapter 8   **You Are the Prize, A Queen with Standards** **73**
You Are the Prize, So Go for the Gold
Your Value is ">" Rubies
Queenly Behavior Begins with a Vision
Queenly Behavior Begins with Loving You
Queenly Behavior Begins with an Environment
Fit for a Queen
Queenly Behavior Begins with Dressing
Like a Queen

Chapter 9   **Introduction to: Your Adam is Awake** **91**
Your Adam is Awake
Chivalry is not Dead, Move Out of His Way
The 40-Day Rule, The Number for Trial
The Father's Role in Your Decision
The Courtship and The Parade Around Principle

Closing   **While You Prepare, Pursue Your Goals and Enjoy Life** **101**

Introduction

I AM A MOM, WHO WANTED TO ANSWER MY DAUGH-TERS' QUESTION, "MOM WHY ARE MEN SO SLOW?"

The question was simple and complex but was the driver which lead the conversations with my daughters and my journey as a Mom to help them understand the answer.

It was important to me my daughters understood their responsibilities prior to saying *I Do*. At the time, my elder daughter was 33 (now 39) and had already experienced the pain of a failed marriage, following the guidelines used in the world. My younger daughter was 20 (now 26) and moving into adulthood as she prepared to leave for the University. Both daughters wanted my help and gave me the green light for some very open, honest and sometimes very direct responses.

The question I asked myself, "Where do I go to get what I need to explain God's process of marriage, the preparation and the intent behind it?" The best resource I could offer them and the foundation of my responses to their questions, was found in our faith. I provided my daughters the insight concerning how men find their mates; and the principles we applied were opposite to the broken process used today. I was pleasantly surprised by my daughters' reactions and responses. Both were excited and expressed continued interest in our discussions. As a result of the information we discussed during those conversations, the discussions generated more questions.

All of us were in awe; my daughters at what they learned and me, at feeling fortunate they embraced what I shared. My daughters loved the simplistic approach I used for some very complex Christian values; some no longer taught, others were overlooked, and new ones discovered during my research. As time passed, my daughters shared more and more with their friends and the results, more and more interest in the information shared. The increased interest inspired me. Eventually, my daughters said, "Mom, you should write a book!" At my daughters' insistence and it was constant, I embraced the idea to write this book.

I finally understood the purpose for this book and my call to write it. It will be important to many. I began to use material written in the draft of this book for counseling singles and married couples. Out of all the writing done in my career, I was nervous about this book project because it will be my first published work.

Although encouraged by my daughters, I continued to look for confirmation. God has a way of sending confirmation concerning His plan, and He sent mine in 2012, through two speaking engagements. Both speaking engagements took place at churches of family friends; Wholly Deliverance Ministries, San Pablo, CA and Resurrection AME, Richmond, CA. This was the perfect time to determine if there was interest in this book.

During the first presentation, I was pleasantly surprised. I recall making my points at the introduction and as I began to give more details; I observed several young people grab their cell phones, quickly run to the front of the church and placed the phones on the front pews to record my message. The audience was fascinated with my discussion concerning why men were asleep and afterwards expressed interest in the book.

The Lady of the church and my friend Demetria Foster said to me afterwards, "The topic of Your Adam Is Asleep Until God Opens His Eyes should be taught to married couples as well". Lady Demetria is now with the Lord, but she had no idea how her words and the young women's actions encouraged me that day. I left the event excited and motivated.

The second event was a mixed group of young and older adults. I decided to share the details about the filters women use to assess potential mates and the danger of what I call *Adam Replacements, Batteries Not Included*. After my presentation, several participants expressed an interest in the book's release date and could not wait for the book.

Your Adam is Asleep Until God Opens His Eyes, will help you discover the deeper purpose for marriage and the work my daughters were challenged to do in order to prepare themselves. You are given access to our conversations with my daughters' and my permission.

Although written based on my conversations with my daughters, men will also find our conversations and topics an eye-opener, in terms of God's expectations of both men and women.

Married couples in need of a reset concerning God's original intent for a successful marriage, will find the foundational teachings a helpful reminder.

Join me as I share what we discovered and read how I answered the most compelling question they asked, "Mom why are men so slow?".

CHAPTER 1

Marriage Was Not Man Made, But God Made

Back to the Beginning

Why start at the beginning? The reason was clear when we considered Genesis as the first book in the Bible and referred to as the "Book of Beginnings" or the "Book of Firsts". The descriptive titles of Genesis provided us clues regarding when things began; how the world began, creation, life, man and woman, marriage and family. Genesis also provided the place to look to discover events which occurred the first time.

I enjoyed the talks with my daughters; my review of Genesis Chapters 2 and 3, the purpose of creation and the events which lead up to the first marriage were important. Founded on our study of Genesis, I am excited to share our discussions, what we learned from the original marriage process, and how it applies today.

The First of the Two Gardens

I understand God is a creative being, and we inherited our creativity from Him. We see God's creativity at work in the

Book of Genesis; He is busy creating a paradise called Eden. God did not plan to live in Eden but designed every detail for a couple who did not exist.

God made meticulous preparations in the paradise designed for the first man and woman. He separated the sea from the land, created light separated by day and night, built a continuous supply of vegetation and seed-bearing plants and fruit, and a host of birds, animals and more. He later created a special place East of Eden, which became the home of Adam and Eve. They did not wear clothes; the section of Eden where they lived had a tropical climate, which kept the area at the right temperature appropriate for living without clothes. God executed every detail with the first couple in mind. God created the first of the two gardens; Eden, the paradise Adam and Eve called home.

God Owns the Patent for Marriage

God owns the patent for marriage; it was not man made, but God made. Why was this point important? My daughters must understand they could not individually take ownership of something which belonged to another. It was important to convey the truth; God owns the process, will open the eyes of their mates in His time, and will bless the union.

The legitimacy of God's patent or ownership of marriage helped to deepen my daughters' trust in the truths I presented. If we believe God owns the patent, we also trust He owns the process. By God's own design, couples come together and are able to fulfill their purpose in marriage because God is made a priority in it.

Women and men around my daughters' ages understood registries for patents, legal rights to a book or an invention, etc. Because my daughters were aware of the patent process, they found it easy to understand and accept God's right

2

to the marriage process. As we began our dialog about marriage from its beginning, we kept all the important facts we addressed in mind.

My daughters and their mates were expected to build their lives together in terms of God being first. By doing so, they will use the blueprint provided in scripture and will follow God's instructions related to their treatment of each other in their marriage union.

Marriage in the Bible, A Book 5 Billion Strong

As we dug deeper, we discovered marriage as a common theme throughout the Bible. The topic of marriage addressed in scripture, which paints a picture of a marriage similar to Christ and his bride. There are three interesting places marriage is mentioned in the Bible; at the beginning, in the middle and at the end. We discussed its location in the Book of Genesis or Old Testament as we looked at the first marriage. It is located in the middle of the Bible scripture where it appears in the New Testament. In the New Testament, Jesus chose to perform His first miracle at a marriage celebration. Located at the end of Bible scripture, we find the last Book closing with the marriage of Jesus (the groom) coming for his bride (the church). We can see from these references and others, God's intention for marriage and how important marriage was and is today. Marriage was designed from the beginning to be the picture of Christ and His Bride.

I chose to close this chapter with credible evidence of the Bible's validity and reputation. I wanted to emphasize its importance in our lives (my daughters and I), and other people of faith; it is our go-to source for everything we want to know about God and His instructions to us. The Bible has stood the test of time; it is our reliable source and the best foundation for our conversations. In closing, here are some interesting facts about the Bible:

Discussions with my daughters centered on references from an old book. Our original Christian guide, the Bible. The Bible was written over 2500 years ago. (www.answers.com/Q/How_long_ago_was_the_Bible_written). In addition, according to the Guinness World Records, the "Bible is the world's best-selling and most widely distributed book. A survey by the Bible Society concluded around 2.5 billion copies were printed between 1815 and 1975, but more recent estimates puts the amount at 5 billion" (http://www.guinnessworldrecords.com/world-records/best-selling-book-of-non-fiction/)

While writing, I recalled an experience which challenged me to respond to someone mocking the Bible. The person claimed the Bible was merely a book written by men; in their mind, the Bible was something man made. You may recall, I said as a Minister and Teacher, in order to expound on the Word, we had to dig deeper. By doing so, the answer to the one who mocked it, was a scripture which says, "All scripture is given by inspiration of God...." (2 Timothy 3:16 KJV). The English word "inspiration" has a different definition than the original Greek language; in Greek it is θεοπνευστος *theopneustos*, literally, "God-breathed". The original scripture actually explains how men wrote the Bible; God breathed upon men of faith what He wanted them to write. The scripture also reserves its deeper revelation for those who believe (Matthew 13:11).

I trust what it says completely and encouraged my daughters to do the same.

CHAPTER 2

The First Man Adam Was Asleep

Asleep or Slow

"Ok, Mom", in my daughters' voices, "Why are men so slow?" My daughters asked this question because they wanted me to explain several things; the reason men did not notice them, the reason they did not recognize hints or clues, and the reason men seemed unaware of their existence or were slow to respond. Our discussions, based on my research, included the revelation I received along the way. My research led me to the discovery of the Genesis Bible story I had known most of my life; but this time, with a deeper understanding. My discovery helped me answer my daughters' question.

My daughters were stunned to find that men were not slow, but asleep. After we looked at the Genesis story, which revealed men were asleep rather than slow, it made sense to them.

We reviewed the scriptures in Genesis Chapter 2 about the first man Adam and the first woman Eve. The story of Adam and Eve created the foundation for our discussions, as the scripture describes why and how God created Adam and Eve, how they met, how and when they married. If the Adam in scripture existed today, he would be called "slow" by my daughters' definition.

The first example of Adam being "asleep" is when he is in the Garden; he spiritually closed his eyes while busy completing his tasks in the Garden. His eyes remained closed, he could see nothing or anyone, because he focused on his obedience to God and on his assigned duties. The second example of Adam being "asleep" happened when God placed Adam physically into a deep sleep. Adam's physical eyes remained closed to the process involved in getting his mate ready. While Adam slept, God created the perfect mate or match for him.

Adam Was Alone, But Was Not Lonely

For a short time, Adam was the only human creation; Eve's creation occurred after Adam. In Genesis 2:20 (NIV), after Adam named the animals, God said "...but for Adam there was not found a help meet for him." The time Adam spent alone is addressed in the previous verses (2:15-17); it was during this time God provided Adam instructions regarding what not to eat and discussed his responsibilities in the Garden. Adam spent his Garden time in fellowship with his Creator and enjoyed fellowship with God; i.e., social interactions and communication on a human intellectual level. He had no one like himself to enjoy this level of interaction; neither did Adam have someone with whom to enjoy physical companionship.

For this brief time, Adam was becoming comfortable with the dominion God assigned to him. Adam exercised the dominion God gave him and named the animals and the animals became whatever he called them. Adam did not become upset after noticing the animals were paired with a mate. Adam knew he was the only human creation, but scripture did not say Adam felt alone or he was lonely. One might assume it to be the case, but I stuck with the facts provided and preferred avoiding a modern-day, 21st century spin on the story.

As I shared this with my daughters, one of the main points about Adam's humble beginnings became clear to them and me; this man was busy in his role and responsibilities. Adam was satisfied in fellowship with God; before there was an Eve. As the first man, Adam performed his assignment in obedience; he discovered his purpose and enjoyed fellowship with the one who made him. He reverenced God, who loved him, and he loved God. Adam did not understand loneliness because of the fellowship he enjoyed, as scripture shows us how God hung around the Garden of Eden with him. Adam was content.

God decided, in His time, that Adam needed someone like himself for human companionship. Again, Adam did not see a need in his life and found contentment in completing his responsibilities.

Adam as we discussed, had it together, but was alone. We can come up with all kinds of scenarios and lists to justify why it was and is not good for man to be alone. Today, there are some dangerous behaviors and addictions men have turned to in the absence of a wife; for example, porn. Also, God makes it clear in His word about physical intimacy outside of marriage. God's position has not changed from the beginning; He said it is not good.

There are so many lessons we can learn from what I shared with my daughters and am sharing with you now. Here are a few points which recaps what my daughters, and I discussed:

The first man kept busy, working; he demonstrated his obedience and commitment to his tasks and fulfilled the call upon his life. I wanted my daughters to understand when their mate revealed himself, like the original Adam, he should be found busy living his life of faith and demonstrating similar characteristics: faithful in his relationship with God, committed to serving God, studies God's Word, prays, goal oriented, strong values, shows leadership, respectful, responsive, demonstrates chivalry – courtesy, loyalty, courage, covering, successful (not necessarily a professional, but successful in what he does), focused – does not straddle the fence.

He did not experience loneliness; and he was not looking for a mate. When their mate arrived, I told my daughters they are to be a surprise event in his life. After God opened Adam's eyes to see the gift he presented to him, Adam expressed excitement. In that moment, my daughters should shake up his busy life; he will recognize my daughter as his mate with the same excitement Adam expressed, in the moment his eyes are opened. At his first look, he will know she is *the One* and she is what he had been missing (more about the missing rib). Remember, up to this point, he did not realize he was missing anything.

His close relationship with God made his life full. A man satisfied and filled in his relationship with his Creator, is the man of faith I hoped my daughters wanted as their covering, provider and protection. God spelled out in his word man's instructions as it relates to his responsibilities as a husband. His responsibility began with his faith and obedience to God as did Adam's. His love for and obedience to God, prepares him to love her, God's gift to him. A man of faith is one who is teachable and is constantly learning to become who God designed him to be; and by doing so, he is able to continue learning after his marriage.

God determined it is "not good" for man to be alone. In discussing this point with my daughters, they became aware of the importance of their role in loving, supporting and providing companionship to their mate. Adam needed a woman's help to achieve all he had been mandated to accomplish; and she was his partner to get it done. Even today, we are reminded in 1 Corinthians 7:9 (NIV) that if you cannot control yourself, it is better you marry than burn with your passion or lust.

Adam needed a faithful, strong, smart, intellectual partner, helper and companion; he could not fulfill his mandates without her. My daughters were very clear about how they will have a huge effect on their mates' success and calling.

Adam, the First Real Alpha Male

I did not want a half-baked, "I'm almost a man" type of guy coming into my daughters' lives. Neither did I want a "Boo" (a title used today) approaching my front door to see my daughters. I believe this is one of the reasons I was given this assignment to write about Adam, which became the foundation for this book; because Adam demonstrated the behavior of a real man of faith or the original Alpha male.

My definition of the original Alpha male is different from the negative description used today. Adam represented all the alpha qualities because he was a product of the original "Alpha and Omega", who is the "beginning and the ending". Adam understood who he was as God's first creation, a man; and it showed in his obedience and how he exercised his dominion.

Adam's example shows us a real man of faith focuses on God first, woman second; God must always be first in his life, just as God is first in hers. Again, although initially alone in terms of a mate, Adam enjoyed fellowship with his Creator. Adam communed, experienced fellowship, connected, conversed and communicated with God; and God in turn, hung around the Garden with Adam. Like Adam, a real man of faith should exhibit the same level of commitment.

9

A Moment of Truth

In Counseling young couples and singles, my husband and I introduced the truth about how Adam put God first. We also share our 44-year marriage testimony to the congregation regularly at True Foundation Ministries; and we share how my husband understands he is second in my life and as his wife, I understand I am second in his life. We both know God is first in our lives as individuals and in our marriage as a couple. It is interesting to witness the reaction of couples and singles, when we share this fact and stress the importance of honoring God first. After sharing, we can see the "ah hah" moment when a couple realizes they must take a back seat to God in their mate's life. My husband and I know there is only one God in our lives and another human cannot fill the role.

A Man Who Prays and Listens

I told my daughters there is nothing more powerful than to hear your husband bombard heaven in prayer on your behalf; I said, your husband will bring whatever you are facing to the throne of God in prayer. A man who can pray God's promises in faith, is a man in fellowship with him. A praying man is powerful and a true priest of his home.

My definition when using the reference "a man of faith" does not include those who simply attends a church or who is busy working in the church; and, in both cases, do not have a personal relationship with God. Although these efforts are admirable, works alone cannot save a person as salvation is God's gift to us (Galatians 2:8-9 KJV). Once saved, he has a relationship with God, and works become a result of His faith. Remember Adam, served God faithfully without hesitation in obedience and reverence to Him. The man of faith enjoys his fellowship with God; and as a result, serves in obedience and reverence to God like the original Adam. My daughters understood my definition.

After talking about a man's relationship with God and his prayer life, we found Adam could hear God and he listened to His voice. Earlier, we discussed how Adam listened to God's voice in Genesis 2:15-18; it tells us Adam received his instructions directly from God.

I shared, like Adam, a man can only lead his home and perform his three-fold assignment (discussed in a later chapter) if he is able to listen to God. He cannot listen to His voice without a relationship with Him.

The man of faith can hear God's voice during prayer and through the reading of the scriptures. If my daughters' mate did not have this relationship, he cannot understand or hear God's voice of instruction concerning his marriage or home. From this talk, my daughters were clear in terms of the man who is not equipped to lead their home.

CHAPTER 3

The First Woman Was Called Good

The Woman Made What Was Not Good, Good!

M y daughters became very intrigued as we discussed the first couple and how they were created and paired. Both daughters reacted in a way similar to the reaction of a person hearing a story for the first time; keep in mind, both daughters were taught the scriptures and this story most of their lives. Their reaction surprised me; at the same time, it excited me.

Eve, the first woman, married a man solely based on who God chose for her. She trusted her Creator completely; she did not act on her faith in Adam, but her faith in God.

The first woman was special. After each stage of creation and at the end of each day, God announced what He created was "good" or "very good". There was only one time God referred to something He created as "not good"; it was in His reference to Adam (the first man) being alone. God and not Adam said "It is not good that man should live alone" (Genesis 2:18 NIV). The Bible says God formed the first man Adam out of dust taken from the ground and afterwards made him a living soul (being NIV) by putting his breath into him (nostrils NIV)

(Genesis 2:6 KJV). God knew exactly what Adam needed and determined to make a "help meet" for him.

The woman came from a man. Although Adam was created from the dust taken from the ground, Eve's creation was different. According to Genesis 2:21-22 (KJV), God caused a deep sleep to fall upon Adam; closed his physical eyes while God created his mate. While Adam slept, God performed what is similar to laser surgery; He removed a rib from Adam and closed up the opening. With the rib taken from Adam, God built or fashioned Eve. By the nature of her creation, Eve was made from man; the rib taken from Adam had his DNA. More on the rib later.

It was important for my daughters to recognize everything about Eve was by God's design: when He built her, why He built her, how He built her, the person He created her to marry and the timing of her arrival. God fashioned Eve to ensure every detail about her was on purpose: her design, shape, nature, purpose, attributes, personality, strengths and values. Eve was physically designed to be the receiver of Adam's love. Keep in mind Adam was asleep while God built her; he did not choose her and he could not change her. He did not know he needed a woman; she did not exist.

God declared in Genesis 2:18 and it is still true today; it is not good for man to live alone. Man was designed to need a mate and woman was God's answer to the need. God chose Eve for Adam and my daughters were expected to accept the same process. God will choose.

She Was Not a Temporary Title

God's action to meet man's need for companionship was not designed to be a short term or temporary solution. She did not represent a temporary role or temporary title such as used today; i.e., Boo or Girlfriend. The woman had a permanent position and title; it was wife and help meet. I encouraged my girls to seek only one title, the permanent one, Wife.

The help meet is not a hired helper, a fill-in or temporary help. Although scripture goes into more detail about a wife's role; and some of those references are addressed throughout the book, a help meet is a title referencing a wife. The first time we find the title help meet, is in reference to God's discussion concerning Adam.

Once we understood God's creation of the very first man and woman, our conversations shifted to preparing my daughters for their goal to be married. This is the place we began our dialogue around a deeper understanding of a term which has been misinterpreted for some time.

It was critical my daughters understood what was involved in becoming a helper and companion to their mate. I did not repeat any of the definitions used at the time, because the majority of them fell flat. I believed there was more on the topic in order to go a little deeper in our understanding of a help meet.

The Helper Who Helps Lead

Going deeper involved examining the Hebrew words for Help Meet found in Genesis 2:18; they are, עֵזֶר כְּנֶגְדּוֹ *ezer kenegdo*. The word *ezer* is translated "help". The word *kenegdo* is translated as "matching" him. Therefore, the simplest definition for the phrase *ezer kenegdo* is a Helper who matches him, a Helper, helps lead. What a beautiful definition for my daughters to use when envisioning themselves in their Queenly assignment as wives.

The help meet's role as a helper is to help lead; however, according to the scripture, there is only one leader who functions as head of the home. The head of the home is the person held accountable for all which occurs in the home.

Proverbs 31 is one of the most referenced scriptures in terms of a more in-depth description of a woman's role; in short, she loves her husband and family, and shows her love by what she does. The Proverbs 31 woman is a business manager, she is strategic and plans ahead, is good at bartering and wise in her purchases, has good character, her husband trusts her, she is valued and priceless. She is the help to help him lead. The perfect analogy is noted below, which demonstrates the role of the help meet in the home. You can see the help meet's role is in God's order of things as well, which we discuss in a later chapter.

A Moment of Truth

There was no such thing as a two-headed Leader. The Leader met and communicated regularly with the Assistants. Together the Leader and Assistants discussed their charge and each contributed to the creation of a plan to meet the required goals. To demonstrate this further, while writing this section, I recalled my responsibilities as a State Administrator. We regularly reorganized and created new programs and processes, which resulted in updates of the organizational chart. When we added programs or hired more staff, those actions drove several other actions; such as, adding more Managers to Lead the new programs and staff, additional work stations, equipment, etc. The Leader is held accountable for the programs and staff. Leaders had the ability to surround themselves with Assistants; however, one person held the title as Leader and was held accountable in the event of poor outcomes or acknowledged when the outcomes were positive.

The Leader met and communicated regularly with the Assistants. There was no such thing as a two-headed Leader. The Leader met and communicated regularly with the Assistants. Together the Leader and Assistants discussed their charge and each contributed to the creation of a plan to meet the required goals. Many tasks assigned to the Leader were executed by the

Assistant. As long as the Leader and Assistant followed the same goals and maintained communication, the two executed tasks agreed upon. It was unimportant whether or not the Assistant possessed skill sets or knowledge the Leader did not; what mattered most, the Leader relied upon and trusted the Assistant and the entire team to get the job done. The Leader, Assistants and team were recipients of the accolades when the outcomes were positive.

The husband and wife team are very similar to the Leader and Assistant role. Both are vital and important in applying similar principles to run their household.

CHAPTER 4

Eve was Adam's Missing Rib

The Man's Lost Rib

I told my daughters they were important to the man because they are the rib he is missing. He searches and looks for only one woman; the one who matches his DNA. It was essential my daughters understood this one point, the mate who finds one of them as his bride, will do so because my daughters matched his DNA. I assured them, their mates are not only looking for them, they will find them.

When my daughters and I discussed this, I wanted to present some important facts concerning the rib and how it applied to their role as wives to their future husbands. It was important to have my facts correct, as in some cases, we discussed the medical make-up of the ribs. Also, critical to our discussion was the accuracy of the information and medical facts presented thoroughly researched; my discussions occurred with my two Registered Nurses (RNs) LOL.

I heard so many crazy reasons used to explain why God created Eve from Adam's rib. One statement said, "She was created from his side so she will always stand by his side." (author unknown) The other statement said, "She was created from his side and not his head so she will understand she is not above him." (author unknown) And, so on. LOL!

I read several crazy explanations; but, for the purpose of our discussions, I wanted to offer my daughters more.

Adam Gave His Rib So Eve Could Exist

In Genesis 2:21 (NIV), the scripture does not say the location of the rib taken from Adam. The scripture referenced what occurred while Adam was asleep. God took one of his ribs and afterward closed up his flesh in that place. Only one rib was taken. Adam gave up a rib so Eve could exist. What people in the Bible did not know at the time, but we understand today, is Adam's DNA was in the rib.

Adam made a blood sacrifice for Eve. You will recall in an earlier reference the next blood sacrifice would be the wedding night. In both cases there was a covenant (agreement, pledge, contract) relationship. Eve will again sacrifice or shed blood, when she delivered their children.

As this discussion unfolded with my two RNs, I shared what I discovered. My first point, both men and women have a total of 24 ribs or two sets of 12 ribs.

If we Google a picture of the rib cage, we find it is made up of 12 ribs on each side. The first seven ribs are called "true ribs" and are connected to the breastbone (sternum). The very first rib in this group of true ribs, is flat, short and C-shaped round and is attached below the neck. Ribs 8-10 are called "false ribs" and are also attached to the sternum or breastbone. The last two ribs, 11 and 12, are called "floating ribs" and are attached to the vertebrae.

All of this information was important to our conversations. Remember, I was having this dialogue with Registered Nurses. The Rib study was also educational for me; taking a rib from Adam had deeper meaning. There are those rare cases where people have been known to have an extra rib, normally located above the first rib around the neck. This being the case, this fact eliminates all those little cliché references regarding Eve coming from a rib on Adam's side. The other fact we learned from the rib is their importance; they were there to protect the internal organs. Our internal or vital organs are essential for survival; we cannot live without them. What a beautiful purpose, to guard and protect the most important organs in the body in order to survive. Adam gave up an important part of himself, which was used to guard and protect his vital organs. Without those vital organs, Adam could not live. As a result of his sacrifice, Adam now has the same duty as the rib, to guard and protect what is essential for his survival, Eve.

Now that we understand the structure of the rib cage, one can assume if the extra rib is found below the neck, this may be the place the rib was removed from Adam. We'll discussed this more later when we discuss why Eve was created for Adam.

What we can surmise so far: God took a rib possibly from the neck where the extra rib is found; ribs were designed to protect the internal organs necessary for survival; and, we understand today the DNA was inside the rib taken from Adam and used to build Eve.

The Rib Must Return and You Are His Missing Rib

Our last point concerning the ribs involved our conversation about the DNA used to build Eve. We talked about the early stages of marriage, the process of "becoming one" was not just a physical one, but also a spiritual one; it is the rib taken which is trying to return to its former place. Becoming one, requires work and effort on both parts so the two learn to operate as one.

I told my daughters I did not believe in the crazy 50-50 rule, because there are times in my own marriage when I could only give a little. For instance, there were moments when I was ill and could only contribute 10%, while my husband contributed 90%. On other occasions, the percentages switched; I gave the 90% and my husband 10%. The percentages fluctuated constantly, as there is no predetermined formula, our goal is to fill in whatever amount is needed at the time. I reminded my daughters about unconditional love and the necessity to respond to their husbands with this kind of love. We learned from God's unconditional love towards us, how we are to love in our marriage. To become one is a lifetime commitment and loving unconditionally will play a major role to overcome the problems that will come to challenge their commitment to their husbands.

I said to my girls, "He will find you!". Once we finished our rib discussion. It was important for my daughters understood God's plan to present the mate he selected for each of them; and expressed his love for Adam by giving him Eve. Adam reacted in excitement to see his beautiful love gift; and did not waste any time to give her his name. He expressed his love for Eve and gave her something which represented a part of himself; it was the name "Wo-man". It occurs today when a husband gives his bride the family last name.

God continues to help point the man in the right direction and it is the man's role to approach the woman. There is only one time in a man's life his eyes will open to his perfect mate. This man may have been a lady's man in the past, or a player all his life, but he will work hard for only one woman; the one God opens his eyes to because He built (prepared) and designed her for him.

He will find you daughters. You are the rib he is missing. You are his DNA match.

A Moment of Truth

My Cousin said he was surprised when his wife told him the two attended the same middle school together. He did not recall his wife in middle school, but she remembered him. She provided detailed information about him; including, the two suitcases he carried daily. He laughed when he realized her description was correct, the two had attended the same middle school. He admitted carrying the two suitcases; one was a brief-case for his school papers and the second case was his musical instrument. Although the two attended the same middle school, he was not aware of her until his eyes opened to her while attending high school. The two have been married 42 years.

A Moment of Truth

My Physical Therapist and I were talking about this book during one of my visits. After I shared the subject of the book, she realized her story also fit the topic and asked me to add her story. She began sharing the story of how she and her husband met; the two recently married. She said a Christian friend asked her to join a Christian soccer team the friend played on. She told the friend she was not a Christian and wanted to make sure the rest of the team will accept her as a team member. The Therapist's friend encouraged her to join, and she did. One day during practice on a field in Albany, California, she saw a guy looking at the team practice. After the practice, the guy walked over to her and offered to help her with her soccer skills; and, the rest is history. The two courted for a short time, she became a Christian, and the two married. They were only recently married at the time of our conversation and moved into a place together the week we had this conversation. During one of their conversations, the two realized they frequented the same coffee shop for quite some time prior to the meeting on the field; he frequented the coffee shop with his friends and she sat by herself completing homework. She confirmed her husband did not see her until his eyes opened that day on the field.

A Moment of Truth

My Niece shared how God brought her together with my Nephew. Their story is compelling in terms of when God destines for a couple to come together in marriage, it will happen, even when obstacles, detours and distractions come along the way.

My Niece says she and her husband met as teens, while she and a friend walked to the mall in Fairfield, California. She says my Nephew drove up in a Cadillac, offered them a ride to the mall and asked for her phone number before arriving to the mall. My Nephew called a week later, and the two began to spend time together; but it ended because she felt he was not settled. A little over three years later, her husband reached out to her through his sister and she discovered his incarceration; they talked for a few months, but it quickly ended. She later married someone else; although the marriage did not last. Over 13 years later and 3 years after her divorce, she reconnected with my Nephew. My Nephew found her again through two mutual associates and pursued her. My Niece admits, at this stage in her life, she was in a different place with a desire for her God-mate and a focus on healing and spending quality time with family. Once again, the two began talking by phone and writing letters; over time their friendship and respect for each other grew. After a few months, both realized they were destined for each other, committed to the relationship and later entered courtship. On June 10, 2017, the two married in a beautiful outdoor ceremony.

Let Him Find His Good Thing

Given our discussions, it was time for my daughters to allow their mates to find them. The original Adam did not search for his Eve; he trusted God to choose and build her. The model God used for Adam is the same used for men today. The man looks for his mate through God, seeks His wisdom, and asks for guidance through prayer. After his prayers, he waits until God reveals her. I encouraged my daughters to follow the same model, in terms of seeking God to confirm *the One*, once he comes. It was important my daughters understood it was critical to hear from God; and they were instructed not to act on the man's confirmation alone.

The Bible says, "Whoso findeth a wife findeth a good thing, and obtaineth favour of the LORD." Proverbs 18:22 (KJV). When I looked at the original meaning of the word *findeth*, it is the same definition used in Proverbs 31:10 (KJV) where the scripture says, "Who can *find* a virtuous woman?" Then Proverbs 18:22 (KJV) uses the next phrase, "...he *findeth* a good thing". The Hebrew word for *good* is *towd*, which means, beautiful, cheerful, fair, fine, glad, graciously, joyful, kindly, kindness, loving merry, pleasant, pleases, pleasure, precious, prosperity, ready, sweet, wealth, welfare, and well favored.

We know God presented Adam's wife to him; by definition his wife was a good thing, and her value to him matched the "far above rubies" criteria in Proverbs 31:10. Eve's attributes and the scriptures we have reviewed thus far, tells of a woman who is spiritually mature, loving, caring nature, takes care of herself, is satisfied with her Christian faith and secure in her success.

The man looks for his wife and only finds her with God's leading.

Like the scripture says, my daughters are the "good thing" their mates are seeking. His eyes remain closed to them and anyone else who attempts to show up. His eyes are not open to them as his mate until God reveals it and opens his eyes; he will simply exhibit the condition my daughters call "slow", because he is asleep until his eyes open. My daughters understood, if the man does not act, the man is not *the One* or it is not their time.

After our discussions, my daughters again understood the process. In spite of any number of hints or flirtatious moves my daughters may make to gain his attention, his eyes remained closed; he will continue to appear asleep until it is time for his eyes to open to the one God has for him.

Wait! Yes, my daughters were instructed not to look for him, but to wait for their mate to find them or wait until his eyes are open. I have to admit there were challenges, but overall both my daughters submitted to this process. In addition, I observed guys who misunderstood their kindness and friendship and saw it as flirty. I encouraged my daughters to be sensitive and aware when this occurred.

A Moment of Truth

To further make my point, I had a shocking experience when I witnessed the state of young women today; although it looked bad, it further demonstrated how young women are not waiting for the man, but showed conduct resembling the negative mannerism men used towards women.

I invited a young man to church; a friend of the family. Sitting in the pulpit I had a view of the entire church and watched the young ladies' reaction as my guest walked through the door and sat down. The expressions I witnessed on the young ladies' faces were like those of thirsty or hungry animals waiting to pounce on him as they wagged their tongues.

As I witnessed this, I thought to myself, "Wow, this is the same negative conduct men show women at times, when a beautiful woman walks into a room full of men." As a woman, I hated when men reacted to me in this way; it made me feel cheap and disrespected. I was shocked to observe young women behave in this way. I wondered why? I questioned, "What has happened to young women, that makes it ok to drool over a young Christian brother as if he was meat?" Their behavior was embarrassing to and for my guest. But, it confirmed why it was important to write this book. I hope this book will become a tool to help provide direction to many.

CHAPTER 5

Intimacy in the Garden

The Second Garden

We discussed the first garden in Chapter 1; also called the Garden of Eden, a garden paradise, or a garden of pleasure. The second Garden in the Song of Solomon 4:12 (NLT); which says, "You are my private garden, my treasure, my bride, a secluded spring, a hidden fountain."

Solomon provided a beautiful description of his bride and she was his personal garden. His description is like the first Garden, which served as a private paradise for Adam and Eve. Solomon also described his bride as a "secluded spring and hidden fountain"; his fountain's purpose is to refresh and quench his thirst. Solomon said his garden or bride was "secluded and hidden", which speaks to his authorization to enter and the only man entitled to access this garden. His description gave us a beautiful analogy of the wife's place in her husband's heart; and was his garden of delight.

My daughters and I compared the two gardens with the chambers used on the wedding night and the chamber used for the royal temple treasures. Like the two gardens, the temple treasure and the wedding chamber were accessible to those given permission. Those without permission could not enter. I call the person unauthorized, a Counterfeit. Counterfeits and boos today do not have permission to access the woman's garden; although many will try to enter this place reserved for her husband.

It was easy to find a story in scripture to help us understand the point in the prior paragraph. We found the perfect story in Isaiah 39. In this story, Hezekiah the king was the only person allowed access to the royal temple treasury. One day the king shows the treasury chamber to his enemies; keep in mind, it was the custom to keep the enemies (or counterfeits) away from the treasure. In this one act, King Hezekiah disobeyed God's order; and because of his error, Hezekiah's enemies later returned and plundered all the treasure. Synonyms for the word plunder are; to ransack, steal, ravage or to rape. As we considered these synonym metaphors, we understood the consequences suffered when an unauthorized person or counterfeit entered the garden bride; i.e., we disobey God's order of things. What was once pure and designed for her husband's delight, is plundered, stolen, raped and ravaged.

My daughters are priceless garden treasures for their future husbands; their value and worth demand respect. If he is not one of my daughter's husbands, he is a counterfeit and unauthorized to have access.

The Exciting Beauty of The Discovery

I spoke about the beauty of the discovery in the above paragraphs. What is it?

Adam and Eve were naked and unafraid; it speaks to their comfort level with each other. They stood before each other with no baggage and accepted each other as love gifts from God; He loved them enough to provide everything they needed in each other and in their garden paradise. Their coming together was pure and beautiful.

It was a blessing Adam and Eve were each other's first and only intimate mate. No one else entered their secret garden or enjoyed what belonged to the two. Both virgins, they had not been with any other person. They did not have physical intimacy until God opened Adam's eyes and presented the two to each other; the two then married. Adam and Eve enjoyed one of the powerful benefits of their marriage; the beauty of discovering each other.

Adam and Eve's experience is the perfect example of the order God ordained. It is a picture of the beauty of discovering the love gift given us when married. They are the perfect picture of how a husband and wife can experience what the two alone can see and experience together. A couple can spend a lifetime discovering new things about each other; and enjoy all the pleasures that entails. It is what I call "the exciting beauty of the discovery".

The beauty of discovery gets missed today and so many can never know its beauty because their chambers were ravaged by unauthorized individuals. Women do not value themselves and many are no longer treated as a value. People today want to test the car first. I told my daughters they are not cars, but precious gifts built for their mates alone. They are not to be shared.

A Moment of Truth

The beauty of discovery reminds me of Christmas time when we open a gift. Inside the gift box is something we did not have before we opened it and we enjoyed the excitement in discovering the gift inside the box for the first time. If the gift is technological for instance, we spent hours discovering the features and the variety of uses; as a game, for dancing, exercise, videotaping, etc. This present allowed us to enjoy it for years to come and was available anytime we wanted to access it.

A Moment of Truth

We were fortunate to begin our married life as two young 19-year-olds. Along the way, we discovered beautiful things we enjoyed about each other; these were not all physical but attributes, habits, things we both appreciated together, likes and dislikes and more. We also discovered big and little acts of love, which have become a pattern for us. As time passed, those discoveries became what we loved the most about each other. For instance, we established a habit we enjoy on Sundays after church services, where we journey to Hilltop for our Sunday coffee date. Sometimes, we will enjoy our favorite bag of potato chips along with coffee and will sit in the car talking about the events from service or people watch. We enjoy laughs and a moment to wind down from a busy Sunday morning and weekend. Our conversations filled us with laughter. There are moments when we people watch and have been fortunate to see a friend or family member. Once home, we continue our talks while we recline in the den; and transition to my husband's favorite TV news channel, which is my cue for a nap.

Moment of Truth

We married young and our income was not much. When my husband asked me to marry him, he bought the best wedding ring he could afford from Milen's jewelry store located downtown (most likely on account). We began with little, but it was special. Our beginning allowed us to discover the beauty in the simple pleasures we enjoyed in and with each other. We could not afford to spend a weekend at a hotel but could create an atmosphere by pretending we were away; with just a picnic basket, a blanket on the floor, music, and playing our favorite board game. We saw our lives grow into where we are today.

Now back to the ring. I did not find a diamond although the papers said there was one. At one point, tried to find the diamond by holding the ring up to the light; I laughed at the results, thinking maybe it was a diamond chip. It was all in fun at my ring's expense, but I cherished what it represented for us. My jokes were not while my husband was present. I did not want him to feel bad about what he could afford. Over time, I realized he was unsatisfied with the ring; over the past 44 years of marriage, my husband made it his mission to buy me several diamond wedding rings as replacements; each time, there were more diamonds and larger sets. His sincere gesture reminded me he wanted to give me his best; as his ability to give more grew, he purchased new upgrades for me. The last ring he purchased, my daughters jokingly described it as "monstrous". It blessed me to give one of my sets, a beautiful marquise diamond, to my eldest daughter when her Adam (Kris) arrived. My plan is to give one of my rings to my youngest daughter when she gets married. Looking back on our lives, I love and cherish the beauty of our discovery and in doing so discovered my husband's heart concerning me.

A Couple with Purpose

Adam and Eve were one of many couples called for a specific purpose; it was important my daughters understood when God presents their mate, they too can expect a kingdom assignment. God has work for the couple to do for his glory, besides marriage being a witness of Christ and His bride (the church).

We talked about how marriage belongs to God as its originator. God directed every little detail when He created the first man and woman. God made a special area for Adam and Eve, called the Garden of Eden. Again, He prepared a Garden for them to enjoy; the Garden had everything they needed. It was meticulous and placed East of Eden. The two had it all.

When we discussed this beautiful picture of God's love for his creation, I reminded my daughters Adam and Eve carried the weight of the responsibilities assigned to them; i.e., caring for the Garden, Adam exercised dominion over the animals, pleased each other and populated the earth. Besides their assignments, they were instructed to cleave or stick to each other. Adam, Eve, the Garden and everything in it had purpose.

I explained this is the same order God uses today. God has kingdom purpose in the two he brings together and blesses the union. God determined when to open Adam's eyes to the Eve. I also shared as married couples we enjoy the benefits of the marriage and all the privileges which comes from the union; but, there is kingdom purpose in the marriages God brings together. My daughters expect the same in their future.

Moment of Truth

Today, there are women who want to marry a man with titles, such as a man in a ministry or a pastor. This is a selfish focus and out of order. We discussed this earlier. At the time I married at 19, I did not set my sites on marrying a pastor; but here I am 44 years later married to a pastor. He was not a pastor at the time we married and it was not my plan, but God's plan. I shared with women often, to be careful what they asked for, if they asked for a pastor as a husband; such an assignment requires Christian maturity and patience to handle the role. The role of a pastor can be a very complicated assignment in terms of the demands of the assignment; if the woman is not mature to handle the assignment, it can become a disaster. The moral of the story, let God choose. A woman does not seek the man, he finds her.

The Two Were One Before They Were Two

There is so much depth to this first couple; so much I cannot share all we discovered in this one book. What I hope you gain from what I have written, is another level of your understanding concerning what God wanted us to learn from the process he used to create and bring them together.

Before Adam and Eve became two, they were one; a rib used to create Eve existed in one person. A rib used to build Eve existed inside of Adam; and the rib before removed, was one with Adam. Once God built Eve from the rib, Adam and Eve became two. Now they are two individuals asked once again, to operate as one; the rib returns to the place taken. Looking at Genesis Chapters 1 and 2, we found Adam and Eve as a couple, a pair, a team; they are the only two humans in existence. We talked about Adam exercising his dominion over the animals when they presented them in pairs. The biblical significance of the first couple was important to explore.

Adam and Eve are two people created, joined in union and instructed to become one in marriage. The biblical significance of the number two is very interesting. Number two can mean union or confirmation of a witness; but the number two can also mean division. We see how division can occur when two people take different sides or have a different opinion.

To understand the charge to become one, we must also look at the number one. Number one is the true definition of unity and competes with no other number. This is powerful! This was not the first example of unity, Adam operated in harmony with God before Eve arrived; the two acted as one in agreement. Adam and his rib were also one. God himself is one, there is no other God besides Himself and He competes with no other; the number One competes with no one.

God's instructions to His first couple prepared them for a successful union. The two were to operate as One; by doing so, it helped them avoid the division which can come from two. They operated as a perfect unit or in unity. We know the Bible teaches there is power in unity and agreement (Matthew 18:19-20).

I cautioned my daughters to remember the process will involve two different individuals, who live in a sin-sick world; and upon their marriage, are commanded to remain committed and operate as One. There is work to do to get there, but it is possible. This is the reason my daughters were to begin work on themselves. More on this later.

Moment of Truth

My eldest daughter expressed, at different stages in her marriage, the difficulties she experienced to maintain unity and agreement. The difficulties experienced resulted from of years living as a single Mom and the challenges of transitioning to living with a husband. We cover the transition process in several places in the book; i.e., testosterone, dumbing down, etc. In my counseling with other couples, I found this was a common struggle for women in my daughter's position, even those who had been single for a long time. Others may express, along with my daughter, how the process of learning to operate as one can be tough; but, it takes commitment. I did not want to give my daughters the impression this was easy; this is the reason we discussed this during my daughters' preparation. I agree it is a challenge; but if my daughters are better prepared, they will understand what to expect. After 44 years of marriage, there are moments that continue to challenge our commitment. It is important to stay committed and to avoid selfishness. The process of becoming one is selfless; unity and agreement is sacrificial.

Moment of Truth

My husband and I were from broken homes when we married; and because of our experiences, we wanted a marriage that was permanent. We did not understand when we made this commitment we would experience difficulties that will challenge our commitment. It was tough to maintain the level of commitment we made in the beginning; and it is the reason for the discussions with my daughters. I hoped to educate and prepare them. My experiences taught me their commitment to their marriage union, like mine, will be tested; however, it is their choice to fight anything which comes against their commitment.

The Two Became One Physically

The Genesis 2:25 (KJV) says Adam and Eve "... were both naked, the man and his wife were not ashamed." The two were naked, bare, and untainted by anything which could cause shame. They did not have experiences, mistakes, hidden agendas or sin to overcome before they could "stand naked" before each other. They had no blemishes on their reputation or character; therefore, issues did not exist to hide from each other. The two were physically and spiritually naked.

My daughters and I talked about the intimacy between husband and wife. It is one of the most vulnerable moments a man and woman share with each other. As we discussed earlier, the woman is her husband's private garden. But what about today's loose opinion of physical intimacy?

We talked about some moral issues which exist today and my position in this conversation was as a woman of faith. I believe what the scripture says; no sex or physical intimacy before marriage. This may sound old fashion, but it is what our faith believes. We talk about how there is beauty in waiting in earlier chapters.

I explained in biblical times if a woman was not a virgin on her wedding night, they stoned her to death. We had a hilarious laugh when we thought about what would happen if women today were stoned for the same reason. We imagined the outcome would be dead bodies everywhere, including inside the church.

This is why this conversation was important to have with my daughters. The discussion was not an effort to condemn my daughters if they were already physically active. As a Mom, it was my job to show love as I presented the truth and point them in the right direction. I left the conviction up to God and His Word. We must talk more and condemn less.

Moment of Truth

My daughters and I had open conversations about self-gratification. At the time we discussed the topic, there were several popular Christian believers in the news, who admitted to some of these problems and shared how they sought medical help. First, I applaud their courage to share with us; I sought the courage for open dialogue about this with my daughters. Again, I presented God's truths, but remained in prayer that God help my daughters accept them. This was the point when my prayers turned into warfare, prayers for deliverance and healing, for God to open their eyes to the dangers, and the truth shared would set them free. Again, as parents we must be careful not to condemn, but allow God's grace to do its work.

Going Deeper, The Blood Covenant

We continued our discussion and decided it was time to go deeper in our understanding about Adam and Eve's pledge or agreement. God commanded Adam and Eve and all married couples to become one; i.e., one in love, physically one, and one in agreement. Adam and Eve were virgins; neither had any physical intimacy with anyone else before their marriage. As virgins, the one they married was the only one allowed to enjoy physical intimacy; remember the garden in the Book of Solomon. Because the two were virgins, they sealed their marriage pledge or covenant in blood.

Adam and Eve had three blood covenants or agreements: the first, when Adam gave a rib so Eve could exist; second, when the two were physically intimate for the first time; third, occurred when Eve had children. The covenant was and is today, a binding promise, pledge, or agreement. We can see, when the woman bleeds during the first intimate encounter with her husband, it makes their covenant a binding contract designed to remain unbroken.

Another blood covenant mentioned in scripture is the rainbow; where God made a binding promise never to destroy the earth by flood again. Later in the New Testament, we find a blood covenant when Jesus shed his blood for us on the cross, as a final sacrifice for our sins. Jesus' unconditional love through His shed blood represented for us a new covenant, pledge or agreement for all his believers.

Once we completed our conversations about God's design, Adam and Eve's examples, the Garden and men, we turned our attention to a focus on my daughters' responsibilities: in preparation, their role as a wife, their marriage, and their personal goals while waiting.

"C" is for Celibacy

My commitment was to maintain patience and loving concern towards my daughters during our discussions; this was our opportunity to be open and honest. I hope those reading these stories will also apply the same level of humility, compassion and grace, God helped me to apply during our discussions.

Christians find it easy, in the name of holiness, to take a negative approach to these conversations. Jesus faced them all; and in all cases, he showed compassion and grace.

At the time of our discussions, I was excited celibacy was popular again. Celebrities promoted celibacy and others who practiced celibacy before marriage; even though many of them had been physically active with others before becoming engaged. I respected their efforts to honor their union; and did not view their efforts in a negative light. I applauded them for trying to do things right. God is a God of forgiveness and second and multiple chances, all our faults covered at the cross. Thank God for His grace.

I wanted my message to remain faith-based. One daughter had a prior marriage experience. I showed empathy towards her, in terms of her personal challenge and the difficulty she faced in taming those desires after divorce. She expressed how difficult it is to listen to married women tell single women to remain celibate while waiting for a mate. She said the married person talking "had shoulders to lay next to at night". In that moment I understood her feelings and sympathized with her and other women in her position. Unless you have walked in her path, it is better to be a support, an encourager, empathize or refrain from making comments where she feels criticized.

My daughter had a valid point; we minimize the difficulty involved in maintaining celibacy once those urges are awakened. We talked about or teach methods to help follow our faith teachings during these moments in a person's life; and it is much better said by someone who walked in their shoes with experience and victory. In these moments, it was important to respect her point of view and show sensitivity, because I was a married woman "with shoulders to lay next to at night".

Moment of Truth

I spoke to the moments when single and how I faced similar challenges to maintain celibacy. I shared my mistakes, and I expressed my resolve or determination during my vulnerable moments, to get it right. It reminded me of an old saying from a member of the Mothers' Board of the African-American Baptist church I grew up in; when you determined to take a stand, she called it "a made-up mind". A "made up mind" is the same as a resolve; a resolve means determined.

In any situation where we resolve to get something done; or to achieve a goal; or to accomplish something, we create steps to get there. What worked for me: I surrounded myself with mature spiritual supporters; had prayer warriors pray a hedge of protection around me and were there to help pray me through difficult moments; kept busy and active in God's work; spent little time alone to contemplate what I did not have; stayed in the Word; prayed for myself; refused to hang around couples and I stayed away from events where couples hung out; romantic movies were out and social media was out. LOL. We did not have much social media back then. But, my daughters understood my point and I hope you get my point too. Today, both daughters shut down social media for long periods of breaks and/or for fasting.

Moment of Truth

One of my Nieces told me about her disappointment in a singles' conference she attended given by a local church. She said the facilitator mishandled and avoided a question asked by a young woman in the audience; the young woman in the audience wanted guidance on how to control her urges. My Niece said the facilitator appeared uncomfortable answering the question and responded by reading a scripture. The facilitator did not offer any suggestions or explain how the scripture applied to the young woman's circumstances. It was a failed attempt, and it avoided the question. The facilitator missed an opportunity to give the young woman assistance which the conference was designed to provide. My Niece concluded that she will not attend any future conferences presented by that church.

Adam Replacements, Batteries Not Included

Virtual means something simulated, fake, or not real; the user is tricked into believing it is real and they respond as if it is real. Like all the other tools or toys used for self-gratification, it is one of the new ways to sin; I refer to them as Adam replacements–batteries not included. At the time I wrote about this, the most popular tool available to women was the shape of a man's private; today, we have virtual tools. Women and men who use such toys as an alternative method to a real mate, choose not to wait for their husband or wife. When someone chooses this path, the person will eliminate the desire for the real thing and develop a preference for the fantasy over what is real. These habits are dangerous and once married, can affect marriage after a period of abuse. As with men addicted to the fantasy world of online porn, these toys are more accessible online, through games and sex shops. Again, this opens the door to an addiction to toys and other virtual or make-believe habits God intended for a woman's Adam or a man's Eve. God created something beautiful between the first man and woman; and much of the teaching is considered obsolete or is no longer taught because people prefer self-gratification.

There were temptations my daughters faced at the time we were talking, which included the dangers of porn addiction and sex toys used for self-gratification available for both men and women. The world has accepted self-gratification as the norm, these are new names for some old sins; i.e., fornication and perversion. Perversion or things the Bible describes as perverted, represent something false, not real, or a fantasy. Earlier, we discussed new names for fornication designed to make people more accepting of them; i.e., sex toys, porn, etc. The fantasy or make-believe or imaginary world involved in self-gratification is the world created from the use of these tools and toys.

Moment of Truth

Virtual technology used for entertainment can also open the door to virtual perversion. For example, I recall a futuristic movie I watched on television. I did not watch the entire movie because I became disgusted when I saw single folks in the movie using virtual reality to satisfy themselves. Every home in the movie had virtual technology. I turned the channel to watch something else. What I found interesting, was how close we are to becoming what I saw in the movie; i.e., I watched a recent news report, which showed developers announcing they created female robots, which will use virtual technology for sexual pleasure.

CHAPTER 6

More About Man, His Role & The Dangers!

Like Adam, A Man Is on the Job

Adam provides us with a great example of a man's responsibilities, as well as prerequisites of my daughters' mates.

Men by nature believe in their role of providing for their families; it is one of their responsibilities, along with protecting and loving their family. I cautioned my daughters not to take this responsibility away from him and respect his role. It is the process. Allow the man room to ensure he has it together before he tries to show interest. Sometimes women can interrupt by, in their minds, trying to help. This is an important walk each man must walk alone; like Adam when he spent alone time with his Creator. Again, my daughters should not pursue him.

Although we began conversations about the men who are slow, you will notice much of the book and later chapters focuses on them. At this stage of our discussions, we addressed what they were to expect of their mates and the dangers to avoid. Earlier, I shared how Adam provided us clues regarding when a man is ready. Adam worked, which equates to a man working by today's standards; he had income, or he was prepared financially. Adam also acted upon the instructions God gave him and in doing so, showed responsibility. We see other women in scripture whose stories are similar; i.e., with Ruth's Boaz, like Adam, he was busy in his assignment when they met and also in Esther, when she met her king.

As discussed earlier, it is an essential requirement my daughters' mates be men of faith, believers, followers of Jesus Christ or born again. It is not my place to argue if he is a seasoned vs a young believer to qualify as a potential mate; we must leave the selection process to God. There was one case I witnessed where a young Christian believer married a seasoned believer and God did a quick work in the young Christian believer's life maturing him over a short period. Through his studies, he gained knowledge, wisdom, and understanding of the scriptures. He soon became a seasoned believer faster than the seasoned believers before him. God matured him and soon after, he became a Pastor.

I reminded my daughters of our conversations around the role of the man in the home and how important it is to have a mate who can hear from God. Without a relationship with God, the home structure would suffer and so will the marriage.

There are many scriptures which support the responsibilities of the two coming together in marriage; two of those scriptures are: "How can two walk together unless they have agreement," (Amos 3:3 KJV); and the warning which says; "Do not be yoked together with unbelievers..." (2 Corinthians 6:14 NIV). The scriptures point to a doomed marriage, when unity, faith and agreement is absent. In order for harmony to exist, the two must commit to the same faith and values, and both possess an ability and maturity to seek God's help and wisdom.

A Man Who Loves God, Knows How to Love

A man who loves God, knows how to love; he cannot love himself, others, or a spouse without the love of God in his heart (1 John 4:7-8). Although we addressed love earlier, there is one scripture often misquoted; it states, "Husbands, love your wives, just as Christ loved the church and gave himself up for her." (Ephesians 5:25 NIV). I provide an in-depth under-standing of this verse in the next paragraph and will expound on it more in the workbook.

A man who loves like Christ, shows he understands his role as the spiritual leader of his home. To love like Christ involves three key roles; Prophet, Priest and King. I wanted my daughters to become familiar with what to expect of their husbands, following the pattern provided us in the scripture. Our discussion about the husband's role, God's command to love his wife, and instructions on how he is to treat his wife, were all designed to help my daughters know what God said and His intent.

God set the high standards he expects husbands to follow. I agree, and so did my daughters, once they understood the powerful way Jesus loves us. The scripture referenced above refers to three key roles; the Prophet, Priest and King: As the family Prophet, he serves as a messenger from God to his wife and children. In his role as Priest, he daily presents his wife, children and needs of his household to God. In his role as King, the husband takes responsibility for the welfare of his family, provides and protects them. The husband meets their needs because he loves and respects his family. As a result of our discussion, both daughters felt more prepared for their mates' arrival and equipped to recognize the real from a counterfeit.

A Man at Dust Level Is Not Ready

A man at dust level is not ready for marriage. For this discussion, we reviewed the creative stages of the original Adam in Genesis 2:7 and learned a few things about Adam's growth and development. After Adam's creation, he accepted his responsibilities and priorities; they were, to become familiar with his purpose, experience fellowship with God, and learn how to apply his dominion. Adam came from the dust and continued his growth as God instructed. I call this stage of a man's growth, the dust level.

Today, a man at the dust level is a reference to a man I call incomplete, not ready or a beginner in his creation stage because God has not finished him. For example, after God created Adam, his creation process continued in terms of what Adam was to learn; i.e., taught the parameters of his responsibilities, and what he owed God through his obedience and fellowship. Thank the Lord the woman was not present to disrupt the process or distract Adam during that time. Dust level is not the time for Eve's arrival. My warning to my daughters about this stage of a man's development, was if a man is at the dust level he has not finished the process, and he is not ready for marriage or to take on the three key roles of a husband. It is important he moves beyond dust level first and my daughters were not to impede his process or interrupt it.

While observing both young and old women pursue men who had not finished the creation process and were at the dust level, I found the majority ended in disaster. Another clue in my statement, the women pursued the man. I did not want my daughters to fall into this pattern and cautioned against this behavior. Remember, in God's wisdom Eve did not exist until it was time; after Adam experienced all the stages we identified above. During this period, Adam's eyes remained closed or asleep.

My daughters, like all women, will grow from God's process of preparing them. While God is getting my daughters' mates ready, He will use the wait time to build and prepare them. Again, taking the time to allow God to prepare Adam during the dust level, while Eve was built.

Another pattern we saw from the first man, was he kept busy as he exercised his authority and dominion. He showed the actions of a man of faith as he completed his responsibilities in obedience to God. We can learn from Adam's example; he was not slothful or lazy, no one forced Adam or pushed him to perform his duties. Adam was obedient. This application, although it refers to a man's ability to provide for himself and his family through his job or work life, also reminds us a man does not sit at a dinner table to enjoy what he did not provide. The scripture says; "a man who does not work should not eat" (2 Thessalonian 3:10 NLT).

Both daughters are professional women, and I cannot imagine or will accept a man who will not work hard to partner with them to put food on the table. Although my daughters are Registered Nurses, I did not require their mates to match or exceed their income levels; we already covered the criteria which were important; i.e., his drive, a hard worker, etc. He must however, meet the criteria and principles we addressed earlier.

A Moment of Truth

When we married, I was one year into my career with the State of California. Two weeks before our wedding, my husband received a layoff letter. My Mother asked me if we should move forward with the wedding, I did so because the layoff was beyond his control. My husband proved to be a great provider, a hard worker, and able to secure work soon after we married. Although I earned more than my husband in our early marriage years, it was always his goal to exceed my earnings. We

49

joked about it a lot because we always operated our household finances by placing both our earnings into a household account. It was unimportant to me which one of us contributed the most to our household account. As time passed, he surpassed my earnings; I enjoyed the proud look on his face when he referred to this achievement. I teased him by saying, "Well, at least you know I did not marry you for money, because you had none in the beginning." LOL!

Warning! Spouse Fixer Upper or Animal Rescue is Not a Wife's Job

Marriage is not my daughters personal project, neither is a "spouse fixer upper" on their job description as future wives. When we talked about this, my daughters knew of women who set out to get married at any cost; without preparation or wisdom they go after any man even if the man had obvious flaws or indications he was at the dust level. These women cannot help the man overcome his flaws or change him; those flaws will not go away because of her. It sounds exhausting just writing about it. My goal focused on preparation of my daughters to ensure a successful marriage. The last thing I wanted for them was a marriage to someone who believe his problems were part of her college thesis or final exam. LOL. I cautioned my daughters to avoid making this mistake.

We continued our discussion about men at the dust level and talked about men willing to accept a woman as his teacher/trainer; or, Mother. Notice I did not say accept her as his wife. Here is another huge mistake, and it is out of order.

Eve arrived after Adam had time to get adjusted to his role; if Eve arrived too soon, she could have become what we are talking about here. Again, it is God's timing and His wisdom which determines when a man or woman is ready. I warned my daughters not to rush this process.

Earlier we talked about men at the dust level and how God did not finish creating and preparing him. Here, is a man who has not accomplished all the steps Adam did; i.e., his alone time with God, he has not figured out his purpose and has not worked in his kingdom assignment. A man needs his heavenly Father's instruction and direction; just as women need it too.

What results when women do this? Women who insert themselves into a man's life as the teacher and trainer, in place of God, will shift to a teacher and trainer role after marriage. The dynamics of the relationship changes from a wife and husband relationship, to one like a mother and son. Eventually the man will hate the arrangement because he cannot find his place as a man; or he cannot wear the pants because his wife has worn the pants from the beginning directing the relationship. We were not called to control the process.

I counseled my daughters to ensure they understood it is not their role to fix a man, who has not matured and at dust level. My daughters are to manage the changes necessary in their own lives, to seek God's help through prayer, and He will bring deliverance in the areas identified. It is the man's job to stand on his own and do the same.

A man rescue is like an animal rescue. I can see the similarities in the friends I am blessed to know; these ladies love animals and taking on the care or the rescue of an animal in danger. My friends will rescue any stray dog or cat, make sure the animal is nursed back to health, and is sheltered from harm. One of my dear friends, will rescue a dog or cat with behavioral issues. One friend explains why the animal developed the issues, almost making excuses why the behavior exists; included in her final assessment, it was not the animal's fault because it suffered from some kind of trauma or mistreatment. Because of the trauma or mistreatment, she was ready to love and nurture the animal until it was better. My friend's work is admirable.

Although animal rescue is a loving calling and needed, the rescue of a man for the same reasons women rescue animals is not appropriate. Women who do this, convince themselves the problems the man has is not his fault. Just like the animal rescue friend, this woman makes excuses for his problems and explains why it is her job to nurture or fix him. The woman makes it her personal goal to help fix his behaviors even if she spends a lifetime with no positive results. She ignores that she is suffering from those same behaviors and believes she is helping him. Although I am not a trained clinician, this person fits the description of an enabler; "a person who encourages or enables a negative or self-destructive behavior in another.". (internet dictionary)

The criteria and process today used to prepare a man, is the same as it was in the Garden. God gets the man ready. The first woman, Eve, was built to be Adam's help meet and was not designed to fix Adam. Adam was not created to change Eve and did not have a say in her design. My daughters cannot fix a mate and their mate cannot fix them. This is not a criterion on a wife's job description. God is changing me daily; and as He does, He alone through His Word is making the change happen. As it will be for my daughters when they become wives.

A Moment of Truth

The friend who loved to rescue animals, rescued dogs and cats. Many of the animals with physical issues; such as, an injured foot or leg, or lost and hungry. Most of the animals suffered with behavioral issues and she committed to helping them. Overtime, after observing the men she had in her life; I realize she accepted men similar to the animals she rescued. She was great fixing the problems of her dogs and cats; but tried to fix the problems of the men she kept allowing into her life and failed. She was great at an animal rescue; but because she made the men her personal rescue projects, with all their flaws and brokenness, she suffered from their behaviors. The result? The relationships ended after several disappointing and frustrating tries.

Another Warning! Temps, Boys, and Boos

To be clear, Temps, Boys, Boos are temporary titles and a Wife is a permanent title and position. The best way to describe the titles Boy, Boo or Temp is to look at their definitions or descriptions. Something temporary, is something which lasts for a limited time, is momentary, brief, and is not permanent. In our discussions, I asked my daughters and myself, why so many women continue to accept a temporary process as the norm? The title Temp describes someone who is interim, which means in the meantime. This is an awful place to be! You are a person's interim mate. You are a temporary stop. Next, I looked at the definition for the word provisional; which means, you are only important for right now. Do you want to be a provisional mate? Yet, these are the definitions or titles accepted today; Temp, Boy, Boo. These are brief, in the meantime and do not hold a position or permanent status.

I worked in a field which involved training, and placed people in permanent or temporary employment. When an employer hired a Temp employee, both the employer and employee agree the job is a short-term hire for a set time. In a temp hire, the employer never makes a promise to the temp employee, that the job will become permanent full-time employment. A Temp hire is for a set time agreed upon at the point of hire and once the time ends, the Temp is let go as agreed.

How tragic! Today, this is what women accept; a short-term arrangement with men, for a set period. When the arrangement ends, with or without kids, there is no obligation to the woman or kids on the man's part. To rephrase the point, a woman enters a relationship with a man who is not committed to her and like a temp employer, the arrangement is for a set time he chooses with no promise of a permanent title (Wife). Although he does not give a verbal statement concerning his temporary status, he does so by his actions and lack of commitment. When the man is finished with your services and with you, the arrangement ends with no obligation on his part. What is even more devastating, he does not change the arrangement if children come into the picture; he made his position clear in the beginning.

Now to address our conversation regarding a boy, the word taken from the word boyfriend. The word boyfriend is not in scripture. The Scriptures speaks about men or a man in terms of marriage. Boys are not qualified to marry.

One of the most ridiculous statements I heard a woman make, was when she announced, "This is my boyfriend; we have been together for five years." I thought, does this woman hear or understand what she told us? She told us this man kept her in a temporary arrangement without commitment or a permanent title for five years, and she accepted it. The man was most likely not committed to her and did not see her as his mate; remember his eyes must open to her. And, he enjoyed the temporary arrangement while he continued to look for the right person.

How can an adult in their 20s, 30s, 40s, 50s refer to a man as a boy for a long period?

We have all kinds of arrangements we call or treat as Christian marriages, but they are not. To rename sin, is not a license to sin; underneath it is still the same old sin. We discussed a few temp arrangements, but others are; shacking, cohabitation, and other temp arrangements, etc.; all of which are temporary housing. These titles are nothing more than new names for fornication. The world system is saying, dress up your living arrangement and give it a new title, make it more acceptable, and rename these arrangements to make it easier to go against what God said we should not do.

Marriage belongs to God and as in our Christian faith, "self" has no part in what God ordained; love is selfless and sacrificial. Women should not accept a temporary title or a temporary home. To expect a positive outcome out of a man who only values a woman as a Temp arrangement is silly. This is important! If a man values a woman as something temporary, his value of her is not worth much. Such a value contradicts the "more than rubies" value God says of women's worth.

Watch Out for Counterfeits

Counterfeit definitions include; forgeries, fakes and imitations. A potential mate can look like he can be the One, but he is not. This man looks like and sounds like an original, but he is not.

This was the moment to stress to my daughters the importance to discern if a man is the One God called for them; men will try to fake it. A counterfeit can present himself as the One by any means necessary; they are expert liars. I told my daughters counterfeits are also sitting in church. I instructed my daughters to apply the same principles with a man in the church building as they would if they met the man in a public place.

It is important for my daughters to use common sense with wisdom, and wisdom which comes from God. They were to watch out for the red flags and I cautioned them to pay close attention to the flags. Counterfeits lie and can sometime be the first to declare God told him you are the One. Let me warn you, this is a lie. He will also arrive quoting scriptures too; again, use wisdom & pray for God's guidance. The parade around principle we discuss in Chapter 9 can help; this group will know if the man tried to hide evidence of a counterfeit. It is easy to date a counterfeit based on the process people use today; they expose themselves to dangers multiple times from dating around.

I explained, the world created a process which leaves women and men broken or with a cut lip to injure each other. This was never God's design for us and it was never my hope for my daughters. Left with a mess when the true mate arrives, he faces the mess my daughters had gone through from those wrong relationships. The true mate will compete with how the men from former experiences treated them. This applies to my daughters as well; men go through wrong relationships and unresolved issues. A counterfeit can be wealthy; however, money is not a criterion for a potential mate. This point reminded me of the Bible story about Nabal in 1 Samuel Chapter 25. Nabal was rich, but his name meant fool; and I did not want a fool, counterfeit, or Boo near my daughters.

I did not want my daughters to waste their time with the counterfeits in this world. I hoped my daughters took a more focused approach, to embrace a practice that will keep their eyes on only one goal; a mate for life, who arrives with his eyes open to them. The goal is a permanent title and position -Wife!

Men Do Not Marry Their Toys

Sometimes during our conversations, we experienced moments when we discussed very serious topics, which were comical. This topic of discussion became one of those moments; my daughters loved this reference. The wisdom from my Big Mom was the perfect fit; she said, "Men don't marry their toys. Even an unfaithful married man will go back home." A play thing or toy is not a wife and most men do not consider her wife material. A toy describes a woman the man uses for his personal pastime and temporary enjoyment; but he does not consider her qualified to become his wife. This woman's circumstances can change, when she changes how she views her self-worth. A man may hang out with this person while he continues to search for the one he wants to commit to.

It was my hope my daughters become comfortable with their value, which was more valuable than a toy. Even though a woman will remain hopeful her temporary title will turn into a permanent one; it does not end well in most cases. Who wants this? I have also seen cases where a man married the toy to appear as if he was settling down; but, after marriage he continued his search for the woman he wanted.

Men, Can See Where You Are

The topic about how men can see where you are, showed my daughters how men know where they are in their lives. This also meant that men can see if they are women of faith or women who attend church; they can see what they believe about themselves.

During our conversations, there were moments I stopped to converse with my husband to get the male perspective; and he confirmed my statement that men can see.

As our talks continued, I reminded my daughters of how God describes the state of our world in His word. The reality, we live in a sin-sick world; and encouraged my daughters to remain committed to their strong faith in God. Through their commitment, they could seek the changes needed in their lives through God's Word. As God changed what was on the inside, the fruit will show on the outside; in their spirit, their demeanor, how they dressed, talked and carried themselves. One test we used, and my daughters found the reality of this so funny, if they attracted Mr. Goldgrille or Mr. Butt-lowPants (fun titles LOL) it meant they had more changes to make on the inside. My daughters agreed and recognized the test was true, they both recalled actual moments related to our test. We enjoyed a big laugh.

CHAPTER 7

Before I Do, Focus on You

Focus on You

I t is easy to stand before an officiant, the person you claim to love, and witnesses to declare "I Do". What is difficult, is the married life you are expected to live after the wedding day; this is true if you did not take time to prepare. My goal was for my daughters to present the best of themselves to their husband.

In Chapter 3, we shared God's original plan for the woman and called her good. But much has changed since the fall of mankind; we live in a sin-sick world. Given the fact that we live in this sinful environment, and in my forty years of ministering to women, to learn of the number of women who do not believe preparation is necessary before getting and keeping a mate. Women in the Bible prepared themselves for years prior, and one year before their marriage. In addition, the Bible provides detailed instructions to women of faith about how we are to conduct ourselves as wives. All of this makes preparation necessary, especially in those cases where the woman applied none of the biblical principles she will need to be the wife God wants for her Adam. The most likely answer to the question, Are you ready? The answer is no. It is the answer my daughters could honesty give.

The first thing I asked them to envision in this process did not involve a mate at all; I directed their attention on themselves. When my daughters understood this focus, they accepted this journey. However, it is not a sprint. The journey involved work and effort on their part to present their best to their mates. My daughters accepted all of this and recognized why setting standards for themselves was important to attract the caliber of mate they deserved.

Time for Preparation

Remember the goal is to present your best self. So much attention goes to the process of the mate arriving, but little attention to what he may find if he arrived at this moment.

As a woman of the 1970's, my generation may be the last of the prepared group of young women. There may be a small remnant of women born after the 1970's who are prepared for marriage, but there are many more who are not. My daughters regularly referred to their own peers as ill-prepared, or in their words, "who did not have a clue". I found this realization sad and disappointing. What made matters worse, is that some of their peers were cocky and believed they were prepared for marriage; but in reality, they were not. I agreed with my daughters, "they did not have a clue".

Earlier we discussed making sure my daughters begin preparations to get ready for their future. I considered this time of our discussions the preparation, instruction and training period. The three letters at the beginning of the word preparation, pre, means before. This is the period before a potential mate arrived; I call this the preparation period. It was important, we transition into this topic, as the process of preparing was more important than the question my daughters asked in the beginning, "Why are men so slow?" The question I prefer they ask and answer, "Am I ready right now?" The answer is no.

We spent time on why men were slow, but it was time to address getting ready when he arrived. It helped us to look at the definition of the word preparation to get a clearer understanding. The word prepare speaks to the time before or to make ready in advance. If my daughters were serious about marriage, I required them to put in the time to get ready. Preparation was important. When we look at the antonyms or opposites of the word prepare, it paints a powerful picture about what it means. The opposites for the word prepare are; unfit, weak, a wreck, disorganized, a neglect, demolished, disturbed. The list is compelling in terms of the preparation we discussed.

Preparation included instruction and training. It was my heart's desire my daughters learn from the experience I gained through my personal journey; which included my mistakes. I believed my personal journey helped shape many of our conversations.

At the time of our discussions, so many women in my daughters age group and older, had forgotten how to prepare; and, there was more focus on the guy and less on their readiness. It surprised me to learn of a woman with the opinion that preparation was not necessary. They complained there were other women who married, who did not prepare. There is no excuse for this kind of thinking and it is unfortunate. The person who takes this position says she does not value herself or a mate enough to present her best to him when he arrives. We do not have the statistics of those who chose not to prepare and if their marriage was a long-term success. I know that we must improve our odds by approaching the process in the correct way. Remember God built Eve just for Adam; He knew the specifications He wanted in her to benefit or compliment Adam. God said she is good.

Moment of Truth

Preparation reminded me of a message I preached at a women's program; the theme, "Lord, Make Me Over". I spoke from Jeremiah 18 (KJV), which refers to an analogy of God as the potter shaping clay, the clay represented us. The analogy is a perfect picture of how important it is for all of us do our best to allow God to mold and shape us; and my daughters in this process. The potter does not work with hard clay (which represents a hardhead or person unwilling to surrender) and will throw it away; he only works with soft clay. Soft clay represents a person willing to surrender to being shaped in whatever shape God wants; this person surrenders to His plan. To further illustrate this point, I looked at the definition of the word potter, means to shape by squeezing; this definition means all of us need preparation (shaping and squeezing) and when God is ready to present him, He wants to present Him with His best work.

Women in scripture considered the preparation stage a serious matter. One book in the Bible which goes into detail about preparation, is the Book of Esther. The book speaks of a woman preparing herself an entire year before the marriage ceremony; keep in mind, she was engaged during this time as engagement was treated the same as a marriage.

Preparation intensified during this stage of her life and focused on her preparing to wed. The preparation included; bathing in fragrances, understanding proper etiquette, cooking training, teachings on how to run a household, family & finances to prepare her for a King. I found this entire preparation process important, given the fact that modern-day women have moved away from any level of preparation, especially since girls are prepared most of their lives for marriage.

The point of this conversation refocused my daughters thinking and placed the importance on themselves, for impartation and elevation. A king looks for his queen. To become a queen or the crown of her husband as spoken of in Proverbs 12:4, my daughters must embrace the characteristics of a queen, prepare as queens, and be the queen before he arrived.

There is a rush to marry with a focus on the wedding day or the event while little attention is given to married life or life after the couple say "I do". Some types of preparation include marriage counseling and other activities which provide the couple tools to use after the wedding. A couple who avoids preparation, is a couple who will begin their marriage ill-prepared. It is unfortunate when couples address problem areas after the wedding, which could have been minimal or avoided had they properly prepared.

As much as my daughters wanted their mates to arrive at that moment, they were not prepared for his arrival. After years of counseling singles and married couples, in most cases the women and men assumed their readiness for marriage but were not ready. My daughters understood why this process was up to God's timing. He knows when they are ready and when their mate is ready. As with Adam and Eve, God presented Eve when He decided Adam was ready. By accepting this process, my daughters embraced that God was in control and He will only do what is best for them, and in His time. To get serious about marriage, the steps included the process involved in preparation to get the outcome they wanted and using the tools God provided to help them enjoy a successful marriage.

Dating in Secret Ignores Wise Counsel

In Chapter 1, we discussed how God is the one who decides our mate, but we need help to confirm him.

How did we get to a place of dating in secret? When dating in secret, this family member prefers to date in private. Some keep their dates hidden from family and those who love and care for them as if they do not matter. I find this practice strange and dangerous; because, dating is not the time to hide, but a moment which should take a village to accomplish. God designed it so that we have the benefit of wise counsel, instruction and training to help.

There are many scriptures which emphasize instruction or wise counsel; because, receiving instruction and training through wise counsel is important. The scripture warns us about the consequences of those who refuse instruction and calls them fools (Proverbs 1:7 ESV). It is unfortunate we have lost the benefit of instruction from those older and wiser. Mistakes happen and pain result from a lack of wisdom and wise counsel. Accepting instruction can help eliminate or minimize those experiences. There are many examples of God's wisdom in the scripture and some in the Book of Proverbs and the Book of Poetry and Wisdom. Here are a few:

"Keep hold of instruction; do not let go; guard her, for she is your life." Proverbs 4:13 (ESV)

"Without counsel plans fail, but with many advisers they succeed." Proverbs 15:22 (ESV)

"Listen to advice and accept instruction that you may gain wisdom in the future." Proverbs 19:20-21 (ESV)

"Where there is no guidance, a people falls, but in an abundance of counselors there is safety." Proverbs 11:14 (ESV)

Scripture reminds us what we can learn from older women, who are to teach the youth. (Titus 2:3-5 NLT). Once a younger woman myself, I recall my effort to receive as much instruction as possible; now that I am the older, I enjoy sharing wisdom with my daughters, while preaching, visiting other ministries and through counseling sessions. I love it!

Moment of Truth

Instructions came at the right time for me, from an 80-year-old Aunt Marie Williams (now with the Lord). Aunt Marie was the eldest member of the Bagby family; and although she is my husband's Aunt, I claimed her as mine and visited her regularly. Aunt Marie had a sweet and caring spirit and a friend to everyone she met. She and I enjoyed our talks; and, although in her 80's, she had a great sense of humor.

I recall a turbulent time in my marriage; so bad I was not sure if my marriage would survive the experience. One day during one of my visits to Aunt Marie's, she sat on her couch holding her dog Pal; as she sat for a moment, our conversation turned serious. She began her statement calling me "Baaaaaaby", as she often did because she could not remember my name; the other times she called me Edie after my husband's Mother. She made the mistake often because she said I looked like her. It did not matter what she called me because it was in love.

As she continued, Aunt Marie talked with me about the difficulties we were experiencing. I had not told her about them, but somehow, she found out. Aunt Marie said; "Baaaabbby! Don't you leave all that work you put into your husband for some other women to come along and enjoy all your work. You better stay in that marriage." Whatever prayers I prayed at the time in my effort to seek direction from God, he answered that day through her powerful words. Aunt Marie give me a view of things I did not consider until she said the words. I thought to myself, "I am not giving the hard work I put into my husband to anyone!" LOL.

I learned it is important to show grace in marriage. God showed us grace on the cross which means unmerited favor or He gave us what we did not deserve. This experience and Aunt Marie's words helped me show grace in my marriage. After she said those words, it made perfect sense; with God's leading, I stayed. We celebrated 44 years together this year. The wisdom we gained through our challenges helped us overcome the next one; the truth is difficulties will come, but if handled with grace, they will make the marriage stronger.

Poor Choices Result in a Mate from the Trash or Falling in Love with a Dog

We looked at poor choices, which can cause a mate to come from the trash or cause them to fall in love with a dog. We included my daughters' self-examination, to find the bad and ugly areas in their lives. These were part of the preparation process. Once they conducted a self-assessment, the two identified several unattractive behaviors which we discussed. I warned them of the outcome if poor behaviors were left unaddressed, further emphasizing this important stage in the preparation process.

Here is a childhood memory, which provides tough words of wisdom from my Mother to one of my brothers concerning his poor choices.

Moment of Truth

I had five brothers and two sisters; and my Mother's hands were full with all the challenges my brothers presented her. My brothers were very handsome and talented men; several sang in popular local groups. My brothers sang in local groups, which became a magnet for girls. Mom, a single Mother, made sure her sons understood what she expected of them in their choices of young women.

I recall the day Mom met a young lady with whom my middle brother associated. Mom found it necessary to be tough and very blunt with my brothers; she asked my middle brother, "Why do you keep looking in the trash can for these girls?" To be honest, Mom was not wrong, the girls he chose at the time seemed raunchy. Maybe this was the reason Mom made her comment; she expressed concern about my brother's future, which is where my brother should put his focus. My Mother's final warning to him remains a memory as well; she said, "Son, you can fall in love with a dog, if you hang around it long enough." In her love for her son, Mom saw my brother more valuable than the women he chose. Mom warned my brother, continuing this pattern will cause him to see his own worth as less valued because of the people with whom he associated; including accepting young women worth less than he deserved.

The characteristics of the women discussed above reminds me of the foolish woman who tears down her house with her own hands, found in Proverbs 14:1 (NIV). She is the type of woman who does not care to tend to the needs of her family and household; she is selfish seeking her own enjoyment. We can understand why my Mother warned my brother about them. This is covered more in my workbook, including what it takes to build your home.

My Mother's wisdom applied to my daughters and all women; there is an abundance of foolish men and women out there. During my many counseling sessions with individuals where abuse was present in their homes, I expressed my position that abuse is a deal breaker. Abuse warrants a specific course of action by the abused, whether at the hands of a woman or man. This is why I pressed my daughters to value themselves first; and by doing so, my daughters set their expectations high in terms of how their mates treated them.

Who wants a dog, a fool, someone with a bad character, mean, rude, or has bad or shady reputation, as a mate? Although my Mother's statements seem tough and very blunt, I wanted my daughters to think about the meaning. Hanging around the wrong people can be dangerous today. I hated to consider the possibility my daughters could fall in love with one of these characters.

Later, I realized my brother's choices reflected what he believed about himself at the time; I know it is true because his choices changed later in life as evidenced by the quality of women he married.

Mom taught all of us how we are judged by the people with whom we associate; the old quote, "guilty by association" is true. 1Corinthians 15:33 (NIV) says, "Do not be misled: Bad company corrupts good character." My daughters did not do everything their friends did; however, most people, specifically men, will believe those friends reflect their character.

Do Not Be the Woman from The Poop Pile

In our conversations, my daughters absorbed the wisdom I shared with them to prepare for married life. Marriage life was a topic no longer addressed or taught. Like today, marriage life is not the focus, but the ceremony receives more attention and detail and little attention was placed on life after the wedding event. I hoped my daughters would use the wisdom I gained from my experience and shared with them as they prepared themselves for their future.

I am reminded of a scripture, which describes a noble wife as a crown to her husband (Prov. 12:4a NIV). This is a great visual of her queenly position. This scripture describes a wife as someone who honors her husband like a beautiful crown on his head. She also respects him as her husband and leader of their family; therefore, her crown becomes a symbol of power. She is like a powerful ornament.

The verse continues with the opposite, discussing a disgraceful woman who is like rottenness in a husband's bones, (Prov. 12:4b NKJV). The latter part of the verse describes how miserable this wife is and the life she created made the man feel like he was living on a dunghill. A dunghill in scripture is the place where they placed the poop and trash. This is a woman or wife who is trashy, wasteful, silly, lazy, loose tongued, and one who ruins the credit and comfort of her husband. The effects of a marriage to this kind of woman is a man who sinks to his lowest as her behavior drains his spirit. What a miserable life.

This person does not meet the definition of a wife; and therefore, the title wife is not the same reference used for the ideal wife or the kind I expected my daughters to become. This man did not seek God in his choice. LOL! The point, my daughters should not have the characteristics of a foolish wife.

Do Not Be the Woman A Man Cannot Lift the Covers On

Those who read this may believe this topic is too personal, but it is a necessary part of preparation. I advised my daughters not to fall short in this area as it is unacceptable if a woman who does not love and cherish her body enough to look and smell her best. It is very important my daughters always present their best; whether at home or out and about. Let me caution, however, this conversation does not include those who may have a medical condition which causes odors. Please show compassion.

Another word of wisdom from my grandmother Big Mom, served as the foundation for our conversations around self-care. Big Mom said, "No man wants a woman he cannot lift the covers on." Big Mom's wisdom related to a woman taking pride in always looking and smelling her best and personal care was important to Big Mom. A man can determine what a woman thinks of herself by her outward appearance and smell.

Big Mom's wise words supported a statement written earlier, concerning the women in the Bible who bathed in fragrances an entire year. Because women bathed for a year, it showed a woman's desire to look, feel and smell her best for herself first. Although men will notice her efforts, it is not intended to impress him, but to help her enjoy the pleasure of expressing her beauty both on the inside and the outside.

My Mother also said, "If you can smell yourself, someone else can smell you too." This is a standard test for myself as I embraced those words and made it my priority to always look and smell my best. When self-care and pampering become a natural part of your daily routine, managing those special times of the month become easy. For instance, my personal items were never in plain view where others can see them. I made sure personal items with an odor did not remain in the house; I placed them inside a bag and carried to the trash can outside. I maintained a clean presence and kept myself in a lady like manner. It is my hope by revisiting our past conversations on this topic, it would serve as a reminder in case they had become lazy. As women, we can become lazy when no one is watching; I wanted them to establish good habits with or without a man in their lives.

Moment of Truth

My husband regularly compliments me on smelling great. I recall a time while travelling for my job, I called my husband as usual to let him know I made it to my destination safely. As we talked, suddenly, my husband stopped in the middle of the conversation and said with excitement, "I can still smell your fragrance on your bed pillow!" We both laughed. However, I quietly laughed because he was not aware I sprayed my pillow with my favorite fragrance, so when he smelled it, he would think of me while gone. It worked! LOL. But, what a beautiful compliment from my husband.

On another occasion, my husband overheard a conversation I was having with my daughters about self-care. After hearing some of my comments, he included his own. He said to them, "Your Mom is right! She always smelled good, morning, noon or at bedtime." My girls both looked at him as he spoke and could tell his sincerity. I thought, "What another sweet compliment."

CHAPTER 8

You Are the Prize, A Queen with Standards

You Are the Prize, So Go for the Gold

First, they must know they are the prize. Before we could discuss men or a potential a mate, before we could address the idea of marriage, and before I could address all the questions they challenged me to answer, it was imperative they understood the power in believing in themselves as the prize. The man is not the prize, they are the prize. Once my daughters showed confidence as the prize and accepted their own value and worth, they could believe in their mate's value too.

While raising our daughters, my husband was the first man to tell them they were special and the prize. While they were young, I reminded my husband regularly how important it was our daughters felt valued by him; he is the first man in their lives and what they learn from their Dad, they will expect from their mate.

I told my daughters to always see themselves as the prize. I recognize there are women who treat men as if they are the prize; however, doing so is out of order. My daughters would love and cherish their mates; however, this conversation focused on giving their mates the opportunity to recognize their value when their eyes opened. Everything I have read concerning the value of a woman in a man's life, points to her as the prize, the crown and love gift from God to man.

I wanted my daughters to reach for better, and better is a permanent title; i.e., a Wife. It is like the focus of a Gold Medalist; this person seeks to win the Gold and not the bronze or silver. An artist looks to become a Grammy winner and not the Grammy nominee. The point, I wanted my daughters to see God's plan for them and to not look for less than. There is more honor and respect for a woman chosen as a wife; because the man chose her, he will place more value on her as his pick.

Your Value is ">" Rubies

We discussed my daughters' value and worth based on God's view. The scriptures tell us a woman's price or value is ".... far more than rubies." (Proverbs 31:10 NIV) or greater than the value of rubies. If my daughters' worth was greater than rubies, it was essential they imagine the cost of rubies at today's prices. By doing this exercise, their understanding quickly deepened, relative to their worth and as a result, set the bar higher regarding the standards they set for their mates. My daughters placed their value much higher than we first believed and much greater than how the world valued them.

I advised my daughters men can see who they are, just by observation. There is something about men and their ability to see how a woman thinks about herself and how she values herself. He can see her worth in her actions, how she carries herself, in how she talks and with whom she associates. I also talked to my husband about this; he agreed men who are not interested in becoming a serious mate, find woman who do not value themselves, an easy target. My daughters' conclusion, "ratchetness, attracts ratchetness".

To further explain, the scripture in Matthew 7:20 (KJV) says a person is identified or known by their fruit; fruit results from their actions or what they produce. My daughters' actions will reveal who they are on the inside and fruit or their character can be seen on the outside.

Moment of Truth

I remember speaking with a young lady about a concern she shared with me. She could not understand why she kept attracting the same caliber of guys; the kind she no longer wanted. I explained, men can see how she valued herself; again, the fruit or changes which occur on the inside is seen on the outside. If she does not make positive changes within herself, she will not have positive fruit on the outside.

This conversation helped my daughters realize the work necessary to prepare themselves. I encouraged them to address their individual issues or problems, to understand their role as a wife, to elevate their own worth as God sees them and to become stronger in their faith. A mate should come along to confirm their attributes rather than convince them their attributes exist. For example: it was unnecessary for my daughters to wait for the man to tell them how beautiful they are, they knew of their beauty; and, it was unnecessary for my daughters to wait for the man to introduce them to love, they loved themselves and were loved by their parents.

My daughters established standards and values before a mate arrived, will become the qualities he will love, respect, honor and adore about them. My statement does not mean my daughters are better than men; but, they were worth a lot more.

Both googled the price of rubies. LOL.

Remember the old saying, "To have anything of value and worth takes work." (author unknown). The quote means it takes work to gain something of value. It is important to know your worth, but also to understand the man should value your worth. This is done in biblical marriages too, where men are required to bring gifts to the girls' parents to show his ability to take on a wife financially, because she was worth it. In addition, the takes a year off from work after marriage; and, his job during the first year to enjoy and please his wife. A man who can do this is one who took the time and made an effort to prepare as expected. Especially if he wanted to marry her.

Although most men today may not have the ability to afford this level of preparation I described above, the approach or expectation remains the same. I advised my daughters their mate should work hard to get them; a practice a real man is proud to do. Some call it the chase, I call it nothing more than God opening his eyes to his mate; and once his eyes are open, he puts in the work to pursue and win her heart.

The scripture tells us he will find you; it says, "The man who finds a wife…" (Proverbs 18:22 NLT). This man is in pursuit of the one he knows is his; he is looking for his missing rib. It is okay for him to feel a little intimidated or feel he has to make improvements in himself to measure up to my daughters' qualities. Remember, his prize or bride is worth it and a real man will do what is necessary to win his wife's heart.

I encouraged my daughters to wait for the man who met their standards. I shared with them I shop for my husband's clothes and how he enjoys it. I love to see him in colors or styles which makes him look handsome. He shops for himself as well but would rather I shop for him as he appreciates my fashion taste. When he gets dressed, he consults me for my opinion about his outfit, suit, shoes, colors or coordinating ties. However, it was not always this way. I told my daughters of the early stages, before and during our courtship where he showed his effort to impress and pursue me.

Moment of Truth

I shared my encounters with my husband, which led to our engagement. The first encounter occurred during our twelfth-grade graduation in June 1972. It was the last day of school and we had our first conversation since our break up two years prior. He walked up and asked to sign my year book. After writing something in my year book, he returned the book and walked away. Afterwards, I looked inside to see what he wrote; it said, "To the woman who will be my wife one day.", along with a poem. I was shocked. I thought, "What are you talking about? We are not talking!" His gesture meant he was thinking about me and included me in his future. Also, later I realized my husband's shyness, which explained some of his behavior.

Our second encounter occurred a few months after graduation. It was August 1972, and I was preparing to celebrate my 18th birthday. Somehow, my husband found out my eldest sister was hosting my birthday party at her home. Without notice or a phone call, he attended my party. He arrived to the party, and I noticed he lost weight. I could see he attempted to look his best, considering he lived on his own. I wondered if he attended my party to check on me, or to see if I was dating anyone. (At this moment I am laughing because my husband is leaning over my shoulder reading this section. His reaction? He read my statement and grinned in agreement.) LOL

As I continued this story, I joked with my daughters about how their Dad dressed at the party. Due to the weight loss, he had a belt which looked as if it wrapped around his waist twice! He wore a wide brim hat, the 70's look. LOL! I am sure he was thinking his hat was the perfect cover for his untrimmed afro although his beard and mustache was neatly trimmed. He wore a leather jacket, jeans and boots; the 70's styled boots with a platform and stacked heel. I laughed inside as I observed what he wore and it was not to make fun of his clothes, but it was obvious he was attempting to impress me. I shared these feelings with my daughters but did not reveal them to my husband until written in this book.

I think my daughters had a bigger laugh at their Dad's expense; afterwards, the two insisted I retrieve my yearbook so they could read the rest of the poem. Once I shared my year book and read their Dad's poem together, we again had a hilarious laugh. On a serious note, my message to my daughters was a powerful one, I provided an honest story, and they saw the actual poem. It was a story about two people they love and respect; me and their Dad.

My daughters recognized the effort their Dad made to impress me; and I appreciated his efforts. I expected my daughters to appreciate the efforts made by their potential mates; my hope is their guys will also show efforts to make improvements in themselves as they pursue them. When my daughters' mates win their hearts, they too will value their winnings and appreciate the caliber and value they are as women. These are the feelings their Dad displayed for me.

You are a designer original my daughters. Like most women I know, my daughters love designer items. Many of their favorites include; purses, shoes, perfumes and clothing. I would love a designer home too. LOL. The reality, a designer original takes thought and planning. The same strategy God used when he created the first woman; an original fashioned by His own hands. The scripture tells us she was built for her Adam. She was what he needed and kept Adam from living alone.

God did not create woman from the wind or from the dust like Adam; she was created from man. He planned the woman's arrival and set the time for her to meet her Adam. It is the same process today. My daughters were to allow God to continue fashioning and building them into who He planned them to be; and they are aware there is only one of each of them.

Queenly Behavior Begins with a Vision

What does queenly behavior look like? It begins with a Vision.

My daughters' faith said they will get married, not they wished to be, but they will be. We began the process of putting their faith into action by returning to an old tool; I presented each a beautiful Hope Box. The items placed inside the box represented their vision for their marriage and married life.

Why a Hope Box? Why a vision? Every business organization, non-profit, church, family or person creates a plan or has a strategy which provides the direction, goals, milestones to success and steps to get there. The Bible tells us to "… Write the vision and make it plain..." (Habakkuk 2:2 KJV). The scripture supports having a strategy, a vision or dream or plan which points us in the direction we desire to go. Without a vision, dream or goal, you will remain in the same place. When there is a vision, we act on the goal, we plan for it, expect it will happen, get ready for it to come to fruition, and take steps towards it. Our actions show why creating a vision is important. A vision works in every area of our lives and it is amazing how we do not apply our faith to our future and seek God for direction. We will discuss more on the vision later.

Like the Hope Chest, the Hope Box represented their belief. As Christians we know "… faith by itself, if it is not accompanied by action, is dead." (James 2:17 NIV) But, what is the point of believing and then do nothing or do not act on what you believe? My daughters understood faith was the key to their ability to build a marriage, home and family; but, before we arrived to these areas, it was necessary to apply their faith to this entire process. It was not worth moving forward if they did not believe God is faithful to keep His promise. We are also taught to operate or act on what we believe; therefore, our preparation and much of our discussion centered on the belief their mates existed and they will arrive as God planned. In the meantime, there was work to do on themselves.

The original Hope Chest was part of an old tradition and a tool representing a woman's vision or dream for her married life. We wanted to take the same approach we use when envisioning our career, or business, etc.; in every case, we map out what we envision and the steps or actions toward the goal. The same idea applies today, but through new tools and creativity. The Hope Box has replaced the Hope Chest, along with the vision board and journal. Although the first Hope Chest was a large wooden chest and used to place the actual wedding items inside; i.e., wedding dress, kitchen utensils, linen and more. Our modern-day Hope Box, uses less space; and thanks to technology, we can use pictures found on the internet to represent parts of the vision. The Hope Boxes come adorned in a variety of prints and colors and are available in a variety of sizes and shapes for every taste and style. We found ours at Hobby Lobby and Michael's.

Whatever the tool, I wanted my daughters to develop a vision of their future wedding and marriage. I presented each with a medium-sized box and encouraged them to place items inside which represented their vision for their wedding, marriage, honeymoon, home, children, career, ministry, etc. I also introduced the Hope Box to a group of single women at the True Foundation Ministry Women's Conference; the participants loved it. Thanks to the internet, both daughters filled their

Hope Boxes with photos of their ideal wedding dress, pictures of their ideal home, and some personal keepsakes representing the children they wanted. My elder daughter placed a picture of a mermaid styled wedding dress, a pair of yellow booties she wore as a baby and a picture of a house inside her box. My younger daughter has pictures of a wedding dress designed by her favorite wedding designer, a Pnina Tornai of Kleinfeld's in New York. She selected the Pavilion as her venue. She has two baby boy onesies decorated in her favorite sports team color and logo in her box.

Moment of Truth

Here is one result of having the Hope Box. My eldest daughter placed a picture of a mermaid styled wedding dress, a pair of yellow booties she wore as a baby and a pink onesie which said "worth the wait"; she did all of this because she waited on God to send her mate and more children. She also included a list of the things she aspired to have in the house they would buy one day. On August 8, 2012, my daughter wore the mermaid wedding dress at her garden wedding, held in the backyard of her in laws. Her daughter and my first grand-daughter came into the world June 2013; she represented the yellow booties and pink onesie. My daughter and husband purchased a three-story dream home in 2017, in a brand-new development.

Elvene Elvie Tampol
AUGUST 8, 2012

Queenly Behavior Begins with Loving You

Love you, while you wait for a mate's love. Loving you, begins with understanding love. A picture of real love can be seen in the story of Adam and Eve; and, it is the love God designed for us all. How does this love differentiate from the watered-down description of love the world uses? My daughters were not to become consumed by their desire for the One; but rather, love and enjoy themselves, and achieve their goals. As they discover this level of love, they will see this love provide a more in-depth view of intimacy experienced between a married couple; and it was crucial my daughters understood real love, apart from expressing physical love. At that time, people used sex as a means to express love; but this view reduced love to nothing more than a hook up without commitment. Overtime, adopting such a weakened view of love, devalued women and men's worth and diminished the beauty of an experience found in waiting.

Understanding real love was important, but more important was that my daughters applied the principles of love to their lives. God says in his Word to love ourselves, our spouses and family, fellow believers and others. Scripture describes real love in 1John 4:7-8, which shows us love originated in God; it says, "God is love" (KJV). The word love in this reference is the Greek word agape, which means it is an unconditional love. The scripture also describes love as a fruit in Galatians 5:22 (KJV); and it is the first fruit as all other fruit must come from love. Love as a fruit comes because of knowing God and living in obedience to Him. We cannot know this kind of love until we know God through his Son. Another fact about love is in 1John 4:18 (NIV) says, "There is no fear in love. But perfect love drives out fear". We need this kind of love to build a marriage and maintain a healthy home.

Besides the word Agape, there are several other definitions for the word love. The others are; Eros is romantic love, Phileo is the love between friends, Storge is brotherly love, family love. However, these definitions do not compare to the higher form of love called Agape. Agape as a higher form of love, describes a love which is sacrificial. We cannot know this love apart from God. This unconditional form of love removes selfishness, pride, and any expectation of the person reciprocating love you give, like Christ does for us. We can see why I wanted to ensure that my daughters learn to apply this selfless love in marriage.

Also, interesting, is that most people practice a conditional form of love, when real love is available. A love based on a condition, require a person do something before the love is reciprocated; it can be a physical attribute, size or the way a person look at the moment. Conditions are superficial and change over time; i.e., my husband had a beautiful head of hair, large curly black afro; today he is still handsome but is almost bald. His condition changed. When we met my measurements were 34-27-37; and, now I am a different size. I will not embarrass myself by revealing my current measurements after kids. LOL! The message from these scenarios? Do not use a person's physical attributes as the only criteria for love; it is conditional and conditions change. Conditions will not last.

I witnessed the unfair treatment of a man who constantly belittled his wife, who could not lose the weight she gained after childbirth. This man subjected his wife to abuse. Why? Because the man wanted the bride he married; the marriage was conditional.

My daughters have strong faith, and as believers, must love and value themselves, and accept who God says they are. God's Word says they are daughters of the most-high God and this was a great place to build their faith and accept their royal status in Christ. In this way, when their mates arrived, their mates will affirm what he sees on the inside. It is a heavy burden to expect a man to carry the responsibility of regularly convincing her that she is beautiful or worthy. Overtime, this will become an exhausting burden for the man; the burden will create problems in the marriage and become too much for him. Exhausted, he will eventually leave. A man cannot fulfill this request; a woman must feel confident about her worth and love herself first.

We discussed God's instructions to love ourselves. If my daughters did not follow the instruction to first love themselves, they could not give love to a mate. A man cannot change what my daughters believe about themselves; each person must change themselves with God's help. I wanted my daughters to become confident of their beauty and worth and encouraged them to accept who God says they are as the truth; anything contrary to what God says is a lie. God says my daughters have these values and more:

Good.–Gen. 2:18 (NIV)

A good thing. – Proverbs 18:22 (KJV)

Wonderfully made.–Psalms 139:14 (NIV)

Far more than rubies.–Proverbs 31:10 (NIV)

Her husband's crown. – Proverbs 12:1 (NASB)

The apple of God's eye. – Proverbs 17:8

Queenly Behavior Begins with an Environment Fit for a Queen

We discussed real love, loving themselves and their complete acceptance of who they were as women, their royal status in God's family and a Queen for their King. It surprised them and they found this funny as we moved into this phase of our discussions. We did not focus our talks on seeking a man to help them enjoy life; but, on the importance loving themselves, taking the time to pamper themselves, achieve their personal goals, reward themselves for their own successes, and fill their pastime with activities they loved.

A queen embraces her beauty, shows confidence, success, happiness, enjoys life, surrounds herself with beauty and everything about her is regal and majestic. She creates an environment fit for a queen. I expected my daughters to enjoy this regal phase as single women; and elevate their standards for the present and their future. This time helped them discover how to make themselves a priority. Love You!

As single women, I did not want my daughters to fall into a rut while waiting for a mate. The waiting could cause the content of our discussions to become lost, forgotten or they could become lazy with their self-care, worth or focus. I knew of women who experienced difficulties in past relationships and as a result, became discouraged; my daughters included. I encouraged my daughters to apply these principles at all times, so they always felt good and valued; because, it is who they prefer to be.

When we discussed beauty treatments and self-care, I explained their personal fragrance or scent is sensual, romantic and attractive. Most will remember a women's scent. I expressed my disdain for poor self-care and a lack of proper hygiene, which is not medical related. Since both daughters are Registered Nurses (RNs), they had a thorough understanding of sterile environments, etc., and can relate to this topic.

I know firsthand how dedicated RNs are by observing my daughters. RNs are one of the hardest working professionals I know. They work long shifts and overtime, to give their patients the best of care. They love what they do. One daughter also decorates the room of her tiny patients in NICU (neonatal intensive care unit). It is our nature as women and modern-day women, to keep busy saving the world, our families, the job and more; as a result, we neglect ourselves. In our conversations, I asked my daughters to see themselves as queens and to see their worth; and to make themselves a priority, take time for themselves, time for special beauty treatments, visits to their favorite lingerie or fragrance stores, massages, facial and beauty treatments, hair salons and spas. This habit will prove useful after marriage and building a family; to remember to take time for themselves even when schedules are busy. It is important to remind ourselves to Love You!

I believed my daughters deserved special treatment, and they adopted the characteristics of a queen at this stage in their lives. My instruction also included creating a queen-like, romantic environment at home.

Besides self-care and special treatments, we discussed exercise and healthy eating; both are great in these areas and have even encouraged me along the way. The two enjoy meal prepping for the week and are active at gyms. My younger daughter now has a personal gym in the garage. Since our discussions, my daughters elevated their choice of fragrances, make up, beauty treatments and more. Both developed habits which showed they applied the principles we discussed; and I could see how pleased they are with their new focus. It is beautiful to witness their transformation.

More assignments related to their queenly status, which involved preparing their home environments fit for a queen. I expected them to enjoy themselves as women; and in doing so, to surround themselves with romantic things. There are no rules which say they cannot be romantic without a mate, in terms of their home environment; i.e., bedroom, bathrooms, bed clothes, etc. Once their mates arrived, they will already be accustomed to a romantic, queenly, royal atmosphere.

My daughters are both beautiful queens and in the process of getting mate ready. By following this exercise, they put into action what they believed they deserved. Their instruction did not focus on money or expensive things, but on the experience; they surrounded themselves with things representing their interpretation of beauty and individual taste. As a result, both my daughters updated their bedroom decor, bathrooms and all the other areas I suggested. One bedroom changed from a college dorm atmosphere to a beautifully adorned black, cream and gold room; while the other is aqua blue, chocolate and off white. Both daughters could feel the difference in the atmosphere upon entering their spaces once they made the improvements.

Queenly Behavior Begins with Dressing Like a Queen

Dress for your future and not your past. The pampering process and queenly home environments happened first, after those changes, they dressed as queens too. There is nothing worse than a woman who dresses like she is unhappy, not blessed and carries herself poorly. This applied to a single or married woman. From my early teaching, I was taught to always consider the person I represented once out in the public; God first, then my husband once married. I expressed this same rule to my daughters and expected them to dress before going out in public; which means well dressed, hair fixed, attire and accessories. It is horrible to see a woman in line at the store looking her worst; pajamas, a scarf tied on her head from the night before. This woman showed that she did not care and did not feel blessed. Remember a woman's appearance speaks to what she thinks about herself, about God, about her husband (if married); and if single, coveys a positive or negative message to other women and men.

Also, Christian appropriate clothing does not mean frumpy attire as my daughters call it.

Moment of Truth

My younger daughter teased her Aunt one day and referred to her attire as frumpy clothing. She continued her assessment by calling her Aunt's attire the "holy saints of Mary and Josephine look"; and said, "they are the wall of Jericho shoes. The shoes leaned so badly to one side as if they had already fallen down". Her Aunt, my daughter, and I could not stop laughing at her remarks. Her Aunt could see why she referred to her clothing in that way and took her criticism as constructive and in love. My daughter enjoyed the humor and reminds her Aunt about this conversation. It revealed that my daughter understood the principles we discussed and why she must be sure she dressed appropriately before going out in public. It blessed me to see she could recognize it when others fail to do so. I also appreciated her Aunt's response.

Once my daughters understood they were to always, always look the part of the queen when out; I hoped it will become habit forming as opposed to dressing-up because they had a date. I instructed them to take time to consider; hair, nails, light makeup, pedicure with sandals, the magic of shades, etc. I would not accept any excuses, considering the many tricks available to women today; enabling us to quickly pull together a look; i.e., one trick is the hair wrap, sunglasses, earrings, and lip stick. I told them, he may be watching. LOL! The basic message is to always look the part because it is who you are; with or without a mate.

Moment of Truth

Although only line staff, I dressed in suits and always carried myself professionally at work. Once I received my first promotion into management, a deputy told me he assumed I had been a manager for two years before my promotion, because of the way I dressed and carried myself. Look like a queenly wife, dress like a queenly wife now; as on the job and in life.

Moment of Truth

I shared my personal bad experience when I forgot the warning to look my best before going out in public. It happened before I became engaged. I walked three short blocks to a grocery store near my house; and, I was sure no one would see me.

I wore a scarf tied into a style. I wore my favorite pair of stars and stripes hot pants (I was not always saved. LOL), a t-shirt and flip flops. Just one-half block remained before I arrived to the store and guess who drove up the street and headed in my direction? My future husband. In addition, he rode in a Volkswagen with two of his brothers. He saw me and got out of the car to walk the rest of the way with me. Embarrassed, I could not talk. I tried to hide my face, but he caught me. I was so embarrassed. I made it a point from that moment, to make sure I dressed appropriately before going out in public. My husband laughs about that day and jokes he focused on my walk and not on what I had on. Really? LOL!

CHAPTER 9

An Introduction to: Your Adam Is Awake

Your Adam is Awake

He is awake, so what does his arrival mean? We discussed what to expect in the process, God's purpose and more in Chapters 1-5. Now that your mate's eyes are open to you, what kinds of adjustments if any will you make to make room for him. This is your sneak peek to Your Adam is Awake Workbook discussion.

Chivalry Is not Dead, Move out of His Way

When your Adam's eyes open, it is time to be ready to move out of his way; because chivalry is not dead; I am happy to report it is alive and well. I encouraged my daughters to allow their men to be chivalrous. This was important because my husband made an effort to ensure our daughters were prepared to care for themselves until their mates arrived; he taught them how to check the oil in the car, look at the batteries, know if the alternator was getting ready to go out, check the tire pressure, change a tire, put a cabinet together and use the tools necessary to get these jobs done.

As single women, my daughters were independent and responsible for their own care. Taking care of themselves also meant they exercised a level of testosterone doing what their Dad taught them. I told my daughters I appreciated their Dad's efforts and agreed it was important for them; however, when their mates arrived, they were to exhibit their feminine side and less of the testosterone. To show too much of testosterone, would be a sign to a man there is no room for him. Men are fixers and you must allow him room to be a man.

The first time I heard the phrase dumbing down, was while watching a tv show. I became curious about the term and searched the internet to determine how it was originally used. According to Wikipedia, the phase is a business slang used in 1933 and defined as, "the deliberate oversimplification of intellectual content within education, literature, cinema, news, video games and culture in order to relate to those unable to assimilate more sophisticated information".

The slang is used today to explain the position of a woman who refuses dumbing down for a man. She is a woman, who refuses to allow her husband to fulfill his role as the man and is determined to take on his tasks because she is just as capable in terms of her abilities intelligence and education.

It is an expression used for a woman who do not feel she has to dumb down to allow a man room to be a man. I can understand a woman's abilities which makes her smart and intelligent as a man and in a marriage, she can perform many of the skill sets a husband can. In my daughters' case, it applies to the things my husband taught them. What is crucial and the wisdom I shared with my daughters, although they may possess the capabilities, it was important they allow their husbands room to be the man in their home. Is it dumbing down? No, it is something else; it is respect for the man you are given. It means, "I love you enough to give you room to be who God created you to be in my home and in my life".

As a woman, married for 44 years, I am speaking from experience. My daughters' husbands should feel they are an important asset to their lives. This is chivalry involved here; his DNA is such that it is necessary he be given the room to show courtesy and respect, to cover and protect, show gallantry, valor and courage. My daughters were asked not to take this away from their mates. To do the opposite and not allow him this room, shows that the person is selfish. This is a loving respectable response, versus a forced one. I shared this with my daughters because it is the behavior they are to exhibit in a loving marriage; we make adjustments because we love the other person. It reminds me of the loving response Jesus showed us in the sacrifice; He responded to our need for a Savior.

Moment of Truth

There are many examples of how my husband shows chivalry in the little and big things he does; he does it all for me. It is his way of showing his love. When we were both working, my husband left for work before my work alarm; before leaving, he prepared a nice hot bubble bath for me. When it was time for me to get up for work, I woke up to the smell of my bubble bath. He knew how to make the water temperature just right, so the water did not lose heat when it was time for me to enjoy it. He shopped for the best bubble bath fragrance and a scent he enjoyed; but I also loved the brand and scent too.

There are other little acts of love, such as observing the many months I spent writing this book during the early mornings or late hours at night. My husband watched as I took care of my grands, helped to chauffer them to school or home, go to my water exercise class, help my nephew and help with ministry work. He was aware when I felt exhausted by observing my face or mannerisms; and oftentimes, encouraged me to take a nap or get some rest. To ensure I followed through, he grabbed the bottle of oil and rubbed my feet until I relaxed and fell asleep. I am grateful for those moments, because his gestures are always at the right time.

I always place my car keys inside my purse once I am home, but at times I forget to do so. In those moments, my husband sets out to locate the car keys for me and once found, he places them in my purse. There are other times when, after spending time downstairs in the den, I can hear my husband as he walks downstairs carrying my phone and charger, expecting I would need them at some point. If I go upstairs for the night or if upstairs for a while, I can hear my husband coming upstairs with his arms full of the things I left downstairs. He does all of this to help me avoid a trip downstairs or upstairs in the case of the phone and charger. I can name so many more. I could have done all of this myself. But, my husband beat me to it. Afterwards, I cannot help but smile thinking how grateful I was for all he does to show his love and concern. It is the little acts of love; and I plan to continue giving him room to be chivalrous.

My husband opens my car door for me to exit the car and opens the door for me to enter the car. We are surprised when we get the stares from both men and woman as they observe my husband doing this. It is both weird and sad recognizing women do not expect this of men.

I volunteer with my Niece in an after-school program she oversees. We have 3-4 boys in a group of about 12 girls. The girls were asked to say thank you to the boys when we assign a boy to hold the door as we exited the class for lunch and on the return to the classroom. I can see how proud the boys were to hear those words from the girls.

Yes, as women we can do it all, but when he arrives, it is important to allow him to be the man. I do not know a woman who does not want a man willing to demonstrate courtesy, gallantry, politeness, attentiveness, loyalty, courage and respect to her. This is what I aspire for my daughters and they should expect from their mates.

In ministering to married women, I met women who tried to hold on to the pants in the marriage; it wreaked havoc on the marriage and made their husband's question why they were in the marriage. I encouraged my daughters to prepare for the transition phase when they are to relinquish the testosterone and allow him room. Remember, it is a loving response and not a forced one.

The 40-Day Rule, the Number for a Trial

Once he arrives, what number should you use as a guide to confirm him? Now I must admit, there are so many numbered plans, goals and phrases used today to measure your progress once he arrives. They range from the 90-day rule, 10-day rules while in a relationship and there are 50-50, 90-10 once in the marriage. My favorite number provided in scripture is used as my guiding principle. I told my daughters that the scripture says the number forty (40) represents a test and trial period.

Since the number forty represents a test or trial, this is the number I asked my daughters to use as the period of time for a man to confirm his intentions. I call it, the 40-Day Rule.

In reality, a man knows his wife at the point of meeting her for the first time; it is the moment his eyes open to her. At the moment his eyes open to her, he knows in that moment she is the One. I told my daughters he may not share this with them right away, but he knows and, in some cases, he may want to continue examining her to confirm what he sees in the beginning. I know of situations where the man expressed these feelings too early and spooked the woman; he did not allow her time hear from God too. I wanted my daughters to hear from God; it is not enough the man knows, God will speak to them too. I told them the man should make his intentions known and be ready to move towards courtship before the 40-day period is over. If he does not, he is asked to move on; he may be a counterfeit.

I recall my daughter testing this rule and the other principles I shared with them; she expressed relief because the 40-day rule helped her avoid wasting time with the wrong person. By using the principles, she could move on without the emotional baggage.

Just for a moment, we considered what Adam was thinking upon meeting his wife for the first time. The first point we can learn from Adam's story, he was not aware of any woman while asleep. While he slept, God was building his wife. Adam did not open his eyes on his own, but it was God who opened Adams eyes when it was time to present the gift he prepared for him. When Adam's eyes opened, he saw her and was so excited he immediately gave her a part of his name; he said, "This is now bone of my bones and flesh of my flesh; she shall be called wo-man...." (Genesis 2:23 NIV). She had his DNA inside of her as she was created from his rib.

Think about how powerful this exchange was for Adam. How did Adam know this woman had a piece of himself inside of her? He was asleep when God built her. It did not take Adam ten years to decide, he immediately accepted God's plan.

The Father's Role in Your Decision

Today, the picture of the garden scene occurs again during the wedding ceremony. At the beginning, before the official ceremony can begin, the Father is asked, "Who gives this woman to this man?" Today the Father gives the bride away, just as God did in the Garden. Just as Adam gave his bride his name, today the Father relinquishes his name so his daughter can take her husband's. During the ceremony, the man declares she is now his mate and gives her his name. The wedding vows are addressed in more detail in my upcoming book entitled, "I Said, I Do".

From this story, one might question how we moved away from this pattern to a process which involves testing the waters multiple times before accepting the one God has designed for us. Some couples have missed each other because of the confusing practice used today. Adam knew upon seeing Eve and knew God determined who he needed. As we adopt this pattern today, we have the benefit of seasoned mentors; married men and women of faith to help guide and prepare us for a successful marriage.

But, before you end with the marriage ceremony, let's back up to see the Father's role during the introduction prior to courtship. His eyes are open, but remember the process is not over. The Father also has a role in determining if this goes further. The most important question a Father asks a man interested in his daughter; "What are your intentions?" It was on the Father's authority that the man is allowed to continue seeing his daughter, because the Father has already found that the man's intention is to move into courtship and marriage; and his decision is determined from the man's answer to that one question. The answer the Father is looking to hear, is yes; and a yes leads to courtship and courtship leads to marriage. If the Father determines the man did not have good intentions, the Father sends him away. There are other methods the Father uses to determine if a man is suitable for his daughter; such as, whether he respects the Father or her parent's rules.

My daughters shared all we talked about with their friends. I encouraged their friends to find a respected male figure who could serve as the father figure who examines a potential mate. It could be a spiritual father/church leader, Uncle, or neighbor. Men understand men, just as women understand women. This process is key. It is the same for the woman who does not have a Mom with whom to have this level of conversation or to make sure she is staying on task with the principles we discuss in the book. She can find a trusted Aunt, Grandmother, friend or spiritual mother/church leader at her local church to help provide guidance.

Today, it is suggested couples also use pre-marriage counseling to prepare them for marriage life and wise counsel from a spiritual church leader. Taking the time to seek wise counsel and preparation will help confirm God's plan for a couple and give them tools for a successful marriage.

Moment of Truth

There are many testimonies from men, who stated they thought their wives were beyond their reach. Here are two stories:

I asked my husband why we did not date in 11th grade after our break-up in 10th grade? His response, "I was saving you for later. I saw what your life was about." He further explained his goal to establish himself before coming back into my life. Once he returned, we courted for a short time. I was not aware he had gone to my Mom to ask permission to marry me and he proposed on my birthday.

My elder daughter's husband admitted to being shy. He said he had to fight his shyness and even hide it, in order to do what was necessary to win her heart. Once he realized his efforts worked, he planned one of the most romantic proposals

I have seen in a long time. He spoke to my husband and me before the engagement; but we were unaware of his plan. For her birthday, my Son-in-Law flew my eldest daughter to New Orleans Essence Festival. He arranged a surprise dinner at one of the oldest restaurants in New Orleans called Antoine's. When the dessert arrived, it was Baked Alaska with a message written on it which said, "Will you marry me?" My daughter sent us a photo. It was so romantic. She said yes.

The Courtship and The Parade Around Principle

It is beyond the forty days and you have moved into courtship or considering courtship. I asked my daughters to listen to God and seek Him to confirm; but also, to use the tools and principles they learned. The parade around, involves introducing the man to key people whose opinion you trust; i.e., parents, family members and spiritual leaders, church members or Pastor. We discussed the Father's role above. But the parade around principle involves parading the man around a larger group, it allows the group to assess him and identify any flags my daughters missed; the parade around is important because their hearts can impede their ability to see red flags the parade around group will notice.

The parade around principle can be applied if a father is not present or if you want more help in making your determination.

Again, this is a healthy way to confirm if he is for you. I do not understand a woman who hides the person she is dating because she does not want anyone to know. Although the parade around principle is another version of the father's role, both are designed to examine the guy; all of it is for the woman's protection. There is beauty in order and all of the actions above are in order.

It was my desire my daughters see the beauty in the order of things as it relates to marriage and the process before their mates' arrival. It was my hope they would come to know the reason for the process as we continued our conversations. It was important my daughters understood the wisdom behind it and the protections within it. Once understood, my hope was it would become important to them too. I am pleased to report, it was important to them.

My daughters were worth more than the current broken process and deserving of the principles we discussed; the principles supported and protected their worth and they discovered how order was beautiful.

I hope you see the beauty in this process too.

Closing

While You Prepare, Pursue Your Goals and Enjoy Life

I wanted no part of this process to consume my daughters' lives; they had goals, passions, aspirations, and to-do lists to accomplish. I encouraged them to keep living and enjoying their lives while applying the principles we discussed. In addition, they were to always keep God first, to continue to serve Him in whatever capacity or calling He placed on their lives; and enjoy their independence, including going out to events, travel and more. For example, it is May 2018 and already this year, my daughter Taylor has traveled to Scotland, Vietnam and has a trip planned to Atlantis in the summer. She discovered a love for these beautiful countries, met great friends and travel buddies along the way.

I encourage those reading this book
to live your life while you wait.
Don't worry, he will find you.

My Family

Look for These Coming Soon

- **Your Adam Is Asleep Until God Opens His Eyes Workbook**
  Designed to accompany the book, Your Adam Is Asleep Until God Opens His Eyes.

- **Your Adam is Awake Workbook**
  A continuation of the book Your Adam Is Asleep Until God Opens His Eyes. His eyes are open and our conversation continues. Building a home and more.

- **Book–I Said, I Do!**
  Most are rewriting their vows but are not taught the beauty of the original. This is my study of the original marriage vows and why they are relevant today.

- **Book – The Mom Code**
  The code us Moms use to avoid uncomfortable conversations with our daughters (or sons). How I eliminated them in order to converse with my daughters freely and intimately.

About the Author

D r. Velma Bagby is a sought-after ordained Minister and counselor for singles and married couples, speaker and teacher. The insight and wisdom she acquired while researching and preparing for the conversations with her daughters, has gained the attention of many others who seek her help.

She is an Associate Minister at her church and is skilled in her ability to present God's Word in her messages and teaching. An advocate for women, who enjoys sharing what she has learned on her journey with others. Dr. Bagby recently completed her Doctorate and plans to continue writing to expand the message of Your Adam Is Asleep Until God Opens His Eyes. She has four additional projects in the works: the workbook for *Your Adam Is Asleep Until God Opens His Eyes*, a second workbook *Your Adam is Awake*, a book entitled, *I Said, I Do!* and a book called *The Mom Code*.

Dr. Bagby is married to her husband of 44 years, Pastor Bruce Bagby of True Foundation Ministries, San Pablo, CA. They have two daughters and two precious grandchildren.

CPSIA information can be obtained
at www.ICGtesting.com
Printed in the USA
LVHW031823240119
605148LV00016B/301